Decolonising Family Violence Legal Intervention Orders in African-Australian Communities

Akuch Kuol Anyieth

Decolonising Family Violence Legal Intervention Orders in African-Australian Communities

palgrave
macmillan

Akuch Kuol Anyieth
Social Inquiry
La Trobe University
Melbourne, Australia

The Centre for the Study of the Afterlife
of Violence and the Reparative Quest
(AVReQ)
Stellenbosch University
Western Cape, South Africa

ISBN 978-3-031-95403-0 ISBN 978-3-031-95404-7 (eBook)
https://doi.org/10.1007/978-3-031-95404-7

The original submitted manuscript has been translated into English. The translation was done using artificial intelligence. A subsequent revision was performed by the author(s) to further refine the work and to ensure that the translation is appropriate concerning content and scientific correctness. It may, however, read stylistically different from a conventional translation.

Cover credit: Roman Lacheev / Alamy Stock Photo

This Palgrave Macmillan imprint is published by the registered company Springer Nature Switzerland AG
The registered company address is: Gewerbestrasse 11, 6330 Cham, Switzerland

Foreword

African communities in Australia constitute a significant and dynamic component of the nation's increasingly multicultural demographic landscape. Their presence contributes to the rich cultural diversity of Australian society, bringing with it a range of social, economic, and intellectual resources. However, despite this valuable contribution, African Australian communities have faced a series of complex and often unprecedented challenges in their efforts to integrate and thrive within broader Australian society. These challenges manifest both socially and structurally, particularly in relation to the Australian legal system.

At the heart of these difficulties are intersecting dynamics shaped by historical, cultural, and political factors. The relationship between African Australian communities and the law is frequently marked by mistrust, misrecognition, and procedural alienation. This is often exacerbated by systemic racism, cultural misunderstanding, and a lack of institutional responsiveness to the specific needs and realities of African migrants and refugees. Furthermore, divergences in social norms, cultural values, and legal expectations—particularly those related to family, community authority, gender roles, and conflict resolution—can create profound dissonance between African Australians and formal legal processes.

These dynamics are deeply rooted in both pre-migration and post-migration experiences. Pre-migration contexts—such as histories of colonisation, armed conflict, displacement, or limited access to justice—significantly shape community attitudes toward legal authority and governance. Post-migration experiences in Australia, including racialisation, marginalisation, and economic exclusion, further complicate this relationship. Together, these factors influence how African Australians perceive, navigate, and respond to legal institutions, often resulting in limited access to justice, underreporting of harm, and heightened vulnerability to legal system failures. Addressing these challenges requires a nuanced, culturally responsive, and decolonial approach that recognises the plurality of legal and cultural traditions informing African diasporic experiences in Australia.

Hence "*Decolonising Family Violence Intervention Orders in the African Australian Communities*" is a groundbreaking and much-needed contribution to the field of family violence intervention and prevention. Drawing on powerful community narratives and rich empirical research, Dr. Akuch Kuol Anyieth offers critical and deeply informed insights into the limitations of current legal frameworks. She compellingly illustrates the urgent need to integrate culturally informed, community-based interventions alongside state-led responses in order to address family violence more effectively.

Dr. Anyieth's decolonial approach challenges the dominant assumptions embedded within mainstream legal and social service systems, illuminating how these frameworks often fail to capture the realities and needs of African Australian families. Rather than positioning culture as a barrier to justice, her work shows how community traditions, values, and mechanisms of accountability can be powerful assets in designing interventions that are both protective and empowering. Her analysis offers a transformative pathway for policymakers, practitioners, researchers, and community leaders who are committed to justice, inclusivity, and real social change.

With deep expertise, scholarly rigour, and an unwavering commitment to justice, Dr. Anyieth shines a necessary light on how systemic racism, migration experiences, and cultural dissonance intersect with family violence and its policing in multicultural Australia. Her book is not only a theoretical contribution but also a practical resource, offering strategies for reimagining interventions in ways that truly respond to the lived experiences of African Australian communities.

This work speaks directly to many of the urgent challenges that African families face within Australia's family violence system today, highlighting the profound gaps between well-intentioned legal protections and their real-world application. It could not have been written at a more critical time, as Australia grapples with questions of multicultural justice, systemic discrimination, and the need for decolonial reform in its institutions.

I wholeheartedly endorse this significant and timely book and commend it to a wide audience across academia, government policy, frontline practice, and community advocacy. *Decolonising Family Violence Intervention Orders in the African Australian Communities* is a critical contribution to building more just, culturally attuned, and effective approaches to family violence intervention and prevention.

Melbourne, Australia Dr. Santino Atem Deng

Preface

My decade-long experience working with many African families in the family violence sector and the courts inspired my academic pursuit many years ago. I came to realise that many African families in Australia grapple with family violence and legal challenges. This led me to question whether solely relying on Western-centric services could genuinely address the complex issues I witnessed daily within the community as well as the legal system. As I transitioned into academia, I recognised the indispensable role of understanding communities' needs alongside the practical implementation of social and criminal justice services. Immersed in academic discourse and the works of influential predecessors, I found comfort in the realisation that, collectively, we are all playing a role in driving the transformation we aspire to see in the realms of family violence, social justice, and systemic change.

Before pursuing a PhD, I spent several years working in various sectors, including the justice system, family violence, youth justice, legal interpreting, and community service and development. Given this background, it is important to share some personal details about my origins and upbringing before delving into the transition from past experiences to my current work on family violence and legal interventions.

I was born in Sudan during the civil war, before the country split into North and South Sudan. Specifically, I was born in the South to Southern Sudanese parents. My formative years were spent in Kakuma Refugee Camp in Kenya, where I often played barefoot on the hot sand under the scorching sun, absorbing the rich narratives of folklore shared by my mother at sunset. This environment shaped my childhood until the age of 14 when my family relocated to Australia in 2005. My deep curiosity and thirst for knowledge emerged from my encounters with violence, trauma, and the unique experiences of living in three distinct yet interconnected worlds—an experience not unique to my family and me but shared by many African Australians, especially those who migrated as refugees through humanitarian programs.

Upon our arrival in Australia, my family and I found that the spectre of war, socioeconomic challenges, and violence had not entirely left us. Instead, we encountered a new kind of conflict defined by ideology, ethnicity, and class in the Western suburbs of Victoria—a state located in the southeastern corner of mainland Australia, bordering New South Wales to the north and South Australia to the west. Here, English became our primary means of communication, yet the ghosts of the past still haunted the future. In the, where we initially settled, English functioned as a second, third, or even fourth language in many households. Vietnamese, Chinese, Arabic, and various African languages predominated as the primary means of communication at home, on the streets, in supermarkets, community spaces, and even playgrounds. These playgrounds often became battlegrounds for children and adolescents who distinguished themselves based on language or accent, which, in turn, signified their ethnic or religious backgrounds. Many engaged in "war games" that began with verbal and physical aggression, escalating into parental disputes and further divisions, perpetuating the cycle of conflict. It seemed as if they were replaying miniature versions of the wars their families had fled from.

We found ourselves residing in one of the lowest socioeconomic neighbourhoods, gripped by trauma, violence, settlement barriers, and self-destructive behaviour prevalent within more established ethnic communities. Despite being in our supposed "safe haven", we grappled with feelings of oppression, far from home and out of place. These experiences, combined with what I observed around me, drove me to seek meaning in my own life experiences and those of my community and society. I was determined to replace uncertainty with a deeper understanding of human behaviour, violence, the dynamics of our new legal system, and trauma within families during and after settlement. My goal was to illuminate the dark corners of human suffering and vulnerability, viewing them not as mere weaknesses but as invaluable sources of learning, understanding, and, ultimately, healing. Moreover, it is necessary to recognise that these families are not dysfunctional or pathological. Instead, they demonstrate resilience as they navigate new pathways to recovery and healthy family relationships.

African Australian communities, particularly the South Sudanese community in Victoria, have garnered significant attention in the youth justice sector. The overrepresentation of South Sudanese youth in the criminal justice system has prompted some investment by the Victorian government. For example, the Department of Justice and Community Safety (DJCS) has supported the South Sudanese Australian Youth Justice Expert Working Group by funding initiatives aimed at helping South Sudanese Australian children and young people to minimise contact with the criminal justice system. This investment acknowledges that South Sudanese Australian organisations are well equipped to provide effective and sustainable programs and services within their communities.

However, research indicates that many justice-involved youth come from households that have experienced family violence (2023–24 Youth Forum Report 1). Family violence within African Australian communities remains an area with little to no substantial countrywide investment from the government. Instead, these issues are often categorised under the broader umbrella of Culturally and Linguistically Diverse (CALD) communities despite the unique challenges related to family violence and the Australian legal system that they face.

Observing instances of severe violence and family struggles piqued my curiosity about how family violence issues were being addressed—or left unresolved—by the legal system within African Australian communities. My aim was to explore the experiences of African Australians and their challenges in navigating a formal legal system vastly different from their customary beliefs and practices.

Over the years, as my interest in family violence deepened, I became increasingly aware of the mounting concerns voiced by many African communities, families, and community leaders. They expressed frustration in community meetings and social gatherings that their difficulties in resolving family violence were being ignored and that inappropriate interventions and prevention strategies were being imposed on victims and perpetrators in their communities. These interventions, rather than mitigating violence, often exacerbated the risk and leave many families doubting the use of legal approaches as tools that can provide safety and prevent family violence within families and communities.

Having shared roots within the same community and coming from a refugee background myself, I had some insight into the experiences of refugees and migrants and their adherence to African customary laws. However, most empirical research on similar topics has been conducted from a top-down, colonial perspective on the legal challenges faced by African communities in Australia. Representations of African Australian communities by white, middle-class scholars—as well as scholars in gender and legal studies—often reinforce stereotypes that depict these communities as "other". Furthermore, the portrayal of people's trauma frequently serves as "evidence of academic merit". This practice not only perpetuates the colonial nature of Western academia but also upholds colonial power structures that prevent individuals from these communities—who are still navigating the negative impacts of colonialism—from conducting research and participating in systems that genuinely represent their collective voices.

In my work within the community, my career, and especially within the framework of this book, my objective was not merely to theorise family violence but to comprehensively examine family violence intervention and prevention, as well as the impact of legal measures such as Family Violence Intervention Orders (FVIOs) with these communities.

I sought to analyse the legal procedures governing these experiences and assess whether these regulations and interventions genuinely benefit the African communities and families they are meant to support.

My aim was to amplify the voices of victim-survivors, appropriate perpetrator interventions while shedding light on the experiences of young people forced to reconcile with the persistent violence within their families. I sought to honour these experiences while striving to understand and theorise violence—particularly family violence—alongside legal approaches for prevention and the remarkable resilience demonstrated by these individuals. To achieve this, I pursued academic training and embarked on a PhD study, which ultimately gave birth to this book. My time in Africa while writing this book greatly enhanced my research, as it confirmed many cultural practices and beliefs shared by my participants. Immersing myself in the social and cultural contexts that shape South Sudanese and broader African worldviews provided me with deeper insights into the transnational dynamics that influence the experiences of African Australians with Australian law enforcement and family violence systems. Writing from within Africa offered a unique perspective to critically reflect on the intersections of culture, migration, and justice—perspectives that might have been less visible if the work had been written solely from Australia. This context not only validated participants' narratives but also deepened the cultural resonance and analytical depth of the text.

Akuch Kuol Anyieth
La Trobe University
Melbourne, Australia

Postdoctoral Research, Fellow at
the Centre for the Study
of the Afterlife of Violence
and Reparative Quest (AVReQ)
Stellenbosch University
Western Cape, South Africa

Acknowledgements I acknowledge the people of the Kulin Nation as the Traditional Custodians of a land that was never ceded. I respect and honour their Elders—past, present, and emerging.

Completing this book has been a transformative and deeply humbling experience. At every stage of this work, I have been guided by a sense of responsibility towards those who have suffered from all forms of brutal colonial practices and family violence worldwide. Above all, this book is dedicated to African Australians in Australia and communities with similar experiences of migration and settler colonialism—the victims and survivors of family violence—with the hope that this book, in some capacity, contributes to the eradication or alleviation of this form of human suffering.

According to a famous African proverb, "It takes a village to raise a child". I feel as though my PhD thesis was that child, and it would never have been completed without the tremendous support of my village. I am deeply indebted to my supervisors, Dr. Anthony Collins, Dr. Kirsty Duncanson, Dr. Emma Russell, and committee member Adjunct Professor Susanne Davis, all from La Trobe University, Melbourne, Australia. Thank you for helping me reach the end of this journey. Your wisdom, encouragement, and mentorship enabled me to remain calm and achieve more than I ever thought possible. You have gracefully guided me through this journey and provided invaluable experiences that I will always cherish.

I am also immensely grateful to the Centre for the Study of the Afterlife of Violence and the Reparative Quest at Stellenbosch University, especially Professor Pumla Gobodo-Madikizela and Dr. Samantha van Schalkwyk, for hosting me as a postdoctoral research fellow and providing me with an intellectually stimulating space to complete this book at Stellenbosch University in South Africa.

Many thanks to Josie Taylor and the team at Palgrave Macmillan for giving me the opportunity to publish this book. Your prompt communication made the publishing process an enjoyable journey.

To all the services, organisations, African Australian community leaders, elders, and faith leaders who assisted in promoting my research during the challenging period of fieldwork and data collection—thank you. I would not have been able to reach the South Sudanese community, broader African communities, and participants without your support and belief in the value of this research.

I extend my immense gratitude to all the storytellers—my participants—who took part in this research and shared their most intimate experiences, perceptions, and emotions with me. You have been selfless and vulnerable in sharing your journeys. For reasons of confidentiality, I cannot thank you by name, but I deeply appreciate your time, memories, and invaluable insights. It has been an honour and privilege to learn from your wisdom, suffering, healing journeys, recovery, your advice, and encouragement.

I want to acknowledge one of my participants who sadly passed away before I could submit my thesis for examination. Her death made the study and this book even more significant to me, as some of the circumstances that led to her passing were linked to core findings in this research—experiences of hardship, family violence, negative encounters with unfamiliar legal systems, and family breakdown. Her loved ones, friends, family, and community will miss her dearly. May she rest in peace.

To my family—your unwavering support throughout this process has helped me maintain my sanity. Your emotional and spiritual encouragement gave me a strength I could not have found anywhere else. During both my lowest and highest moments, your love and belief in me gave me the courage to persevere.

Competing Interests The author has no competing interests to declare that are relevant to the content of this manuscript.

Contents

Abbreviations

CALD	Culturally and linguistically Diverse Communities
FDV	Family and Domestic Violence
FV	Family Violence
FVIO	Family Violence Intervention Order
PTSD	Post-Traumatic Stress Disorder

1
Introduction

Introduction

This book investigates family violence legal intervention orders at the intersection of African Australian cultural practices and beliefs surrounding family violence. Like many other Western countries, Australia hosts a significant population of migrants and refugees from African nations. Given the growing African population in Australia, the complexities between African approaches—embedded in cultural practices—and Australian approaches—rooted in colonial legal interventions—make this community an ideal case study for understanding how these interventions intersect with cultural practices in non-Western communities.

Individuals from African Australian communities come from multifaceted backgrounds, with intricate practices and approaches to social, legal, family, and personal matters. Their experiences with various systems during displacement, in refugee camps (for those who migrated as refugees), and throughout the migration process have both challenged and shaped their cultural and traditional practices, influencing their legal consciousness—specifically, how they perceive themselves before the law (Juuk, 2023).

A. K. Anyieth, *Decolonising Family Violence Legal Intervention Orders in African-Australian Communities*, https://doi.org/10.1007/978-3-031-95404-7_1

Within the broader context of African Australian communities, this book argues that Family Violence Intervention Orders (FVIOs) are often negotiated within cultural practices and beliefs system, which can impact their enforcement and monitoring. This may lead to a reluctance to seek help or intervention from services due to fears surrounding the disclosure of family violence experiences and the consequences of having an FVIO in place. Therefore, the book contends that, due to numerous operational, systemic, and cultural challenges, FVIOs operate within the shadows of African Australian customs and cultural practices in ways that complicate their original intent and effectiveness as a legal intervention and as tools for protection.

This book addresses this knowledge gap in two ways: first, by examining cultural and traditional approaches to family disputes, such as family violence, within African customary law practices; and second, by exploring the experiences of respondents and applicants of family violence intervention orders within African Australian communities, particularly the South Sudanese community. It assesses the impact of these orders on the community and investigates the role of cultural practices in navigating and negotiating family violence intervention orders. FVIOs serve as the core focus of this research, examined through an intersectional decolonial approach. This provides the basis for the collection of empirical data through semi-structured, in-depth interviews with applicants and respondents of family violence intervention orders. A decolonial approach is used to enrich understandings of legal protection through FVIOs in family violence matters and to incorporate shared African cultural approaches and practices, enabling more appropriate and nuanced tools for family intervention and prevention.

Though broadly situated within the context of African experiences in Australia, the specific experiences analysed in this book—and informing the chapters presenting the empirical evidence—are drawn from in-depth semi-structured interviews with South Sudanese Australians. Despite prior studies on the challenges faced by African Australian settlers, little is known about the unique encounters of applicants and respondents within the context of family violence legal interventions, distinct from their home countries. However, it is important to acknowledge that African Australian communities are not homogeneous, though they share common experiences that deserve attention in this book.

Therefore, studies examining the unique challenges within African Australian communities should first situate themselves within the broader African Australian shared experience of colonialism, conflicts, migration, settlement challenges, and everyday life experiences in Australia before honing in on specific groups. It is important to first acknowledge shared historical backgrounds, cultural values, practices, and settlement challenges, as well as the common perceptions of Africans in Australia and the approaches taken to address these challenges before, I discuss the role of family violence and intervention orders.

Key Concepts

It is important to first present key concepts and definitions relating to family violence, intervention orders, and African Australian communities in this earlier section of the book. Introducing these key concepts and definitions ensures that readers are equipped with the necessary understanding to engage with the subsequent analysis. This foundational knowledge is crucial as it contextualises the broader issues of legal protection and cultural adaptation, setting the stage for a more in-depth exploration of how African Australian communities interact with the legal frameworks designed to protect them.

African Australians

African Australians are individuals of African descent living in Australia (Abur, 2023). This community comprises migrants, refugees, and descendants from various African countries. They contribute to Australia's multicultural landscape through their diverse cultures, languages, and traditions. While actively participating in various sectors, the African Australian community often faces unique challenges, including racial profiling by law enforcement, discrimination, and negative representation in the media (Abur, 2023). These challenges will be discussed further in Chapters 2 and 3.

South Sudanese Australians

South Sudanese Australians are individuals of South Sudanese descent or birth who reside in Australia (Juuk, 2023). Most South Sudanese Australians arrived as refugees, fleeing the Sudanese civil war, particularly between 2001 and 2006 (Juuk, 2023). They have settled across various states and territories, with the largest populations in Victoria and New South Wales. The South Sudanese Australian community is one of the most prominent African communities in Australia (Abur, 2023).

Intersectionality

"Intersectionality refers to particular forms of intersecting oppressions, for example, intersections of race and gender, or of sexuality and nation. Intersectional paradigms remind us that oppression cannot be reduced to one fundamental type, and that oppressions work together in producing injustice" (Hill Collins, 1990:18). Coined by Kimberlé Crenshaw (Maschke, 1997), this concept emphasises that overlapping systems of power give rise to unique forms of discrimination and disadvantage. These complexities cannot be fully understood by examining each identity category in isolation because there is no such thing as a single-issue struggle because people do not live single-issue lives (Dudley, 2006). This book uses intersectionality as a framework to explore the complex and layered experiences of African Australians, especially regarding family violence, legal intervention, and systemic marginalisation. By adopting an intersectional lens, the book reveals how African Australian women, men, and families navigate their experiences of violence and the legal system while dealing with their cultural identities, migration histories, and experiences of systemic exclusion.

Family Violence

Family violence refers to a complex array of violent, abusive, or aggressive behaviours that occur within a family (Tarpey-Brown et al., 2024). It is a situation in which one person often seeks to exert power and control over another. This violence can take many forms, including physical, emotional, psychological (including coercive controlling behaviour), and financial abuse, among others (Fitz-Gibbon & Walklate, 2023; Segrave et al., 2016). The various forms that family violence can take are a testament to its complexity. It not only affects those directly involved but also has a significant impact on children and other family members, often leading to long-term psychological, economic, and emotional consequences (Fitz-Gibbon & Walklate, 2023).

Family Violence in the Context of African Families

In the African context, family violence refers to any form of abuse or harm that occurs within a family unit, affecting its members physically, emotionally, psychologically, or economically (Fitz-Gibbon & Walklate, 2023). This includes various types of violence, such as physical, sexual abuse, economic abuse, and neglect (Fisher, 2013; Mungai & Gitau, 2019; Robinson et al., 2025). Family dynamics, cultural beliefs, and practices significantly influence the definitions and perceptions of family violence in African societies (Fisher, 2013). Unlike the traditional Western definition, which often focuses on the immediate family, the African definition recognises the importance of communal relationships (Mungai & Gitau, 2019). It includes extended family members and individuals who are considered part of the family through social ties rather than solely biological connections.

Trauma

According to van der Kolk (2014), trauma is a psychological and emotional response to profoundly distressing or disturbing events that overwhelm an individual's ability to cope. It can result from experiences, such as violence, abuse, war, displacement, or loss, and it may have long-term effects on mental, emotional, and physical well-being. Trauma can be experienced by individuals or entire communities; in some cases, it can also be intergenerational, impacting communities over time (Atkinson, 2010).

According to James et al. (2022), trauma in African Australian communities, trauma refers to deep psychological and emotional distress, often compounded by intergenerational factors, resulting from experiences such as war, forced migration, racial discrimination, systemic marginalisation, and family separation. This trauma is frequently shaped by pre-migration conflicts, refugee experiences, and the challenges of resettlement, which intersect with structural inequalities and cultural displacement (James et al., 2022). These factors significantly affect the well-being of individuals and communities.

Australian Family Law

Family law in Australia addresses legal matters related to family relationships, including marriage, divorce, child custody, property settlements, and domestic violence[1]. It is primarily regulated by the Family Law Act 1975, which provides a framework for resolving family disputes (Walklate et al., 2017). Family law is a complex field that encompasses both federal and state legislation, with each case varying significantly based on individual circumstances.

Family Violence Intervention Orders

A Family Violence Intervention Order (FVIO) in Victoria, Australia, is a legal order designed to protect individuals from family violence (Reeves, 2021). It can be requested by anyone experiencing or at risk of family violence, including physical, emotional, psychological, or financial abuse.

[1] Read Family Law Act 1975 Sect. 1.4AB Definition of family violence etc.

An FVIO can impose specific conditions on the perpetrator to ensure the safety of the affected person (Reeves, 2021). These conditions may include prohibiting the perpetrator from approaching or communicating with the affected person or their children, as well as restricting access to shared homes or specific locations (Campbell et al., 2021) To obtain an FVIO, the affected person must typically apply to the Magistrates' Court, where the court will assess evidence of the violence or risk of violence. If granted, the order remains in effect for a specified period, and the applicant can apply for a renewal if necessary (Reeves, 2020, 2021). An FVIO is meant to provide immediate protection while also guiding those involved through the complexities of family violence situations, including safety planning and access to support services.

Conceptualising Colonialism

Colonialism has historically been characterised by the domination of one group over another. This includes occupying or settling land, economic exploitation, political control, coercive cultural changes, and the establishment of systemic structures that have sidelined Indigenous structures, knowledge, and ways of boing (Boonzaier & Van Niekerk, 2019). In recent years, scholars have categorised colonialism, including its modern forms, into four main types: settler colonialism (large-scale immigration and establishment of colonies), exploitation colonialism (primarily focused on extracting natural resources and labour from local populations), surrogate colonialism (where a foreign power grants rights to a population not originally present in the territory), and internal colonialism (occurring within state borders) (Gabbidon, 2010; Glenn, 2015).

Historically, colonialism was reinforced by stereotypical representations of Indigenous populations in regions such as Africa, Australia, Canada, the United States, and Latin America. These populations were often portrayed as backward and in need of modernisation, a concept that Edward Said (1995) referred to as "Orientalism". Colonial powers operated under the belief that they had an obligation to "modernise" Indigenous populations according to Western or Eurocentric standards, defining acceptable norms in various areas, including religion, culture, law, health, and social relations (Quijano, 2000; Smith, 1999).

Christianity, in particular, was frequently used to justify colonial interventions. Indigenous faiths, dispute resolution methods, and belief systems were condemned as less enlightened and in need of correction (Hardin, 2002). As a result, Indigenous knowledge and ways of understanding the world were devalued (Bhargava, 2013). Additionally, colonialism was rooted in the belief that Europeans were superior to Indigenous populations, primarily due to racial differences. This belief firmly linked colonialism to racism (Fanon, 1963) and supported the imposition of formal governance systems, such as common law, in regions like Africa and Australia.

Ongoing Colonialism and the Role of Coloniality

Discussions about the legacies of colonialism must advance while acknowledging the varied experiences of colonisation and decolonisation, which unfolded at different paces in each location in the world (Craib, 2017; Shohat, 1992). The terms colonialism, coloniality, decolonisation, and decoloniality are often used interchangeably, yet they carry distinct meanings. In this book, I am guided by the concept of decolonisation, which, in this context, refers to the dismantling and reform of power and legal structures embedded within colonial institutions, such as the legal system.

Efforts to Decolonise

There is growing recognition of the need to decolonise societal structures and processes (Abimbola, 2019; Boonzaier & Van Niekerk, 2019; Khan et al., 2021; Singh et al., 2021; Zakumumpa et al., 2023). While some define "decolonisation" purely as a political process referring to independence from colonial powers (Naicker, 2023), I align with critical scholars who use the term more broadly to describe it as a theoretical process on one hand and as a practical process of the dismantling of structures and legacies of colonialism on the other (Betts, 2004; Smith, 1999).

Emerging from the resistance of activists against colonial rule, decolonisation has become a crucial framework for challenging and dismantling colonial legacies across various domains, including research, humanitarian aid and development, legal system, academia, and global health (Peace Direct, 2021; Singh et al., 2021; Smith, 1999). For instance, decolonising research involves strategies such as embedding critical reflexivity into research methodologies (Thambinathan & Kinsella, 2021) and ensuring the meaningful involvement of communities and local actors in designing research and interventions (Mannell et al., 2021) that are align with their unique needs.

However, I acknowledge concerns raised by scholars such as Krugman (2023), who argue that the concept of decolonisation has been co-opted by elite institutions in the Global North, leading to its dilution into a liberal reformist framework. Rather than engaging in the deep structural transformations that decolonisation demands, these institutions have turned it into a fashionable term or "buzzword", often used in ways that preserve existing hierarchies rather than dismantling them. Krugman (2023) argues that his "buzzwordification" of decolonisation means that instead of fostering genuine systemic change, it is frequently reduced to symbolic gestures, such as diversifying curricula or acknowledging colonial histories, without addressing persistent material and structural inequalities. In such contexts, decolonisation becomes more of a performative act than a revolutionary process it was intended to be.

This concern partly informs second half of Chapter 2, which examines the intersection of inequalities and experiences of violence faced by African Australians. Addressing these intersecting inequalities and experiences of violence within the broader African Australian communities is a critical starting point for genuine decolonisation. The decolonisation process must first recognise the wrongs of the past. These wrongs are still present, influencing the present, and could impact the future if not challenged by actions that lead to real change.

Research Context

Evidence indicates that imprisonment rates among African Australians, both adults and youth, have increased (ABS, 2017; Department of Premier and Cabinet, 2018a). Individuals born in South Sudan have the highest imprisonment rates in Australia after Aboriginal and Torres Strait Islander peoples (Australian Bureau of Statistics [ABS], 2014; Department of Premier and Cabinet, 2018a).

The high rates of contact with the criminal and civil justice systems have been linked to social and economic challenges experienced both before and after migration (Armytage & Ogloff, 2017; Coventry et al., 2015; Forson, 2019; Shepherd & Spivak, 2020; Shepherd et al., 2018). While it is crucial to examine African Australians' interactions with the criminal justice system to better understand the issues affecting the community, it is equally important to consider the role of violence within families. This includes addressing family violence and the legal interventions designed to combat it, such as Family Violence Intervention Orders (FVIOs), which serve as both preventative and intervention measures.

Legal and non-legal family violence intervention and prevention strategies are based on the belief that family violence does not discriminate. To some extent, this is true, as family violence occurs across all communities. However, research such as Campbell et al. (2021) shows that it is more severe in certain sections of society and manifests in diverse forms across different communities and individuals. Cultural beliefs and practices within specific communities often influence how family violence is experienced and responded to. For instance, Milos (2011) and Juuk (2023) found that in the South Sudanese community, cultural beliefs and practices regarding family violence intervention and prevention sometimes contradict Australian family law and legal interventions, exacerbating family breakdowns.

Research Questions

This research has two main objectives. First, it investigates and explores the experiences of individuals applying for and responding to family violence intervention orders within the South Sudanese community. Second, it examines the impact of these orders within the community and seeks to understand the influence of cultural practices in navigating and negotiating family violence intervention orders, as well as cultural preventative measures.

Additionally, this research aims to contribute to existing knowledge on family violence, intervention orders, and their effectiveness, particularly within the South Sudanese community and other African communities with similar backgrounds. To achieve these objectives, a decolonial qualitative research approach was employed, utilising semi-structured, in-depth interviews with 20 South Sudanese individuals who have first-hand experience with family violence and family violence intervention orders.

The study explores how South Sudanese individuals navigate and negotiate family violence intervention orders, whether these orders serve their intended purpose as a form of intervention and protection within South Sudanese Australian community, and how shared African cultural practices and interventions can be recognised and incorporated to help reduce family violence. These research questions formed the core of the study and were integrated into 13 semi-structured, open-ended interview questions.

Decolonising Methodologies

Decolonising research involving formerly colonised peoples requires a departure from rigid Western structures and principles. Embracing the "messiness" highlighted by Tuhiwai Smith in the third edition of "Decolonizing Methodologies" (2021) allows researchers to respect and integrate the cultural contexts, beliefs, and ways of knowing the communities being studied (Smith, 2022). It is this "messiness" that led to the generation of rich data for this research.

It has been observed that communities with former refugee backgrounds often have a well-founded fear of participating in research (Pernice, 1994). This fear can arise from various factors, such as uncertainty about how research findings will be used, concerns about being portrayed negatively or ungratefully, and apprehension stemming from past experiences with unethical studies conducted by anthropologists, legal authorities, and various systems in the African context. Therefore, I had to take time to build meaning relationships within the community, frame interview question in a conversational manner, and kept participants engaged and informed about the progress of the project until completion. The participants were also given a copy of the thesis.

Building Trust

To mitigate the well-founded fear of participation in research within the South Sudanese community, trust had to be a crucial element employed in conducting decolonial research. Discussing sensitive topics like family violence and court orders, such as intervention orders, can be challenging within any community, especially one that has been under the scrutiny of the Australian media for alleged crimes (Coventry et al., 2014). Therefore, trust was a fundamental structure that underpinned this research in its entirety. Trust is a vital indicator of healthy relationships in the South Sudanese community. Prolonged experiences of violence, colonialism, and oppression have contributed to a lack of trust in scientific research within minority communities like the South Sudanese. Hence, there is a need for a cultural revolution in research, achievable through prioritising community engagement as a strategy to build trust in the research process. According to Liamputtong (2010), trust-building between the researcher and the researched in a decolonising research process is vital, and its development should be based on values of respect, reciprocity, collaboration, and cooperation. Therefore, in this research, trust is inseparable from vulnerability because establishing trust goes hand in hand with protecting the vulnerable against exploitation.

Respecting Cultural Beliefs and Practices

Cultural norms and practices, such as the symbiotic relationship between young individuals and elders in South Sudanese culture, were thoroughly considered during the preparation and execution of the interviews (Pittaway et al., 2022). In South Sudanese culture, social relationships are structured by age. Therefore, the significance of age in these social relations shapes the interaction between seniors and juniors. In this relationship dynamic, it is customary for the younger (junior) person to ask questions while adhering to cultural cues (McLean, 2005). These cues encompass demonstrating respect by inquiring about the well-being of participants, their families, and extended families, avoiding direct eye contact during discussions, standing up when greeting an elder, and walking alongside them as they exit the interview room. Incorporating such practices was instrumental in eliciting a positive and truthful responses. The questions were posed in a non-judgemental tone, conveying curiosity, empathy, and a willingness to learn, rather than positioning myself as an authoritative expert on the subject matter (Bogdan & Biklen, 1992). This approach recognises that participants are the true experts when it comes to their own lived experiences and cultural knowledge.

Language (Code-Switching)

South Sudanese individuals often come from non-English speaking backgrounds, and even those who have learned English in Australia can experience challenges in comprehension and articulation, particularly in settings where technical terms are used, such as discussions about family violence and the legal system. When conducting interviews with participants from South Sudanese backgrounds with limited English proficiency, I needed to consider the potential for misunderstanding, interpretation errors, or loss of meaning and context. To overcome the language barrier, I initially prepared all recruitment materials in English and then translated them into Dinka and Arabic. I provided detailed explanations, including the consent forms and information packs, in the participants' chosen language (with most selecting Dinka and English). During the interviews, I orally asked questions in the participants' chosen language, personally transcribing them without relying on a translator for the non-English transcriptions. However, I remained aware that meanings could be lost or altered in translation and code-switching, so I occasionally turned to my first language, Dinka, to unravel the underlying meanings of certain words. This approach helped distinguish between the textual meaning (word-for-word translation) and the contextual meaning (placing words within their significance in the given context) (Laviosa et al., 2017). These processes of using more than one language in one inquiry can be complex and messy. However, the benefits of participants' self-expression without having to speak English fluently outweigh the complexities and messiness.

In addition to language considerations, the decolonial methodology also involved an openness to the use of code-switching by participants during interviews. While most interviews were conducted in English (many with African accents), participants were given the flexibility to code-switch when they felt that certain questions would be better answered in their native language. This was particularly helpful when English terminologies limited the intended meaning they wanted to convey or when specific Dinka or Arabic Sudanese terminologies did not have direct translations in English. Code-switching refers to the practice of using more than one language within a sentence or discourse (Sahib et al., 2021; Shay, 2015). It is a natural occurrence among multilingual speakers who share two or more languages (Shay, 2015). Code-switching extends beyond speech and includes situations where individuals shift from one accepted vocabulary, cadence, style, or set of rules to another (Shay, 2015). Even in the writing of this thesis, code-switching is evident, as the style is tailored for academic readability and comprehension rather than the way I would verbally explain the study to my family and friends. During the interviews, code-switching occurred naturally, allowing participants to find the most appropriate words to express themselves, thereby increasing their comfort and rapport with me as the researcher, considering that behaviour and language are often culturally influenced (Sahib et al., 2021; Shay, 2015). The acceptance and encouragement of code-switching, and the comfort it provided participants in expressing themselves with fewer language limitations, further underscore the importance of adopting a decolonial approach in this research, especially given that this is almost an everyday way of communication within the South Sudanese community.

To effectively research vulnerable groups, several strategies can be employed. Firstly, it is crucial for researchers to invest time in getting to know the participants and establishing a strong rapport (Liamputtong & Ezzy, 2005). Rather than assuming that the community is burdened with "social problems" or "deviant identities", researchers should recognise that participants possess unique lived experiences and specialised knowledge that may differ from their own (Dickson-Swift et al., 2007). It is important for researchers to accurately represent the perspectives of participants while maintaining integrity throughout the research process (Dickson-Swift et al., 2007). By doing so, research can not only provide validation but also contribute to empowering vulnerable communities, which is, in part, a central objective of this research.

Another effective way of demonstrating respect towards participants and building rapport is by providing something in return, either to the participants themselves or to the community as a whole (Liamputtong & Ezzy, 2005). Liamputtong emphasises the importance of reciprocity and giving back as a means to establish trust with vulnerable participants. This can involve sharing useful information or promoting social change as part of the project (Liamputtong & Ezzy, 2005). In this research, physical incentives were not offered to participants. Instead, appreciation for their participation was expressed, and debrief phone calls were conducted to provide feedback during and after the research, which held significant value for both the participants and myself. Additionally, some participants reached out to me weeks after the interviews, seeking assistance with social services. I helped them by providing referrals and connecting them with services I had encountered in the past, which built and maintained trust. These gestures were highly appreciated by those who sought support. For instance, one of the mothers I interviewed asked if I knew of any free local homework clubs in her area. I conducted a search and found two options, one operating at her local library and another at a community centre. I contacted her and shared the details of both homework clubs. She expressed immense gratitude when her school-aged children began attending the club. Nurturing such post-interview relationships within ethnic communities, especially within the South Sudanese community, is of utmost importance and should be maintained whenever feasible.

Time Management: African Time

In Australia, many Africans are known not to adhere strictly to Western time, giving rise to the concept of "African time". African time is a cultural norm characterised by a more flexible perception of time compared to Western cultures, which emphasise punctuality and setting appointments (Marlowe, 2012). According to Marlowe (2012), African time is subjective and influenced by various factors such as ongoing engagements, the nature of the subject matter, familial obligations, and responsibilities. Consequently, many South Sudanese individuals may not strictly adhere to deadlines, necessitating an adjustment to Western concepts of time and appointment-keeping. This reinforced the need for a decolonial approach in this research, allowing for engagement with participants' ways of functioning and practices while respecting these cultural norms.

As an insider, I, the researcher, being a South Sudanese woman who has been academically trained in the West, encountered challenges related to late arrivals to interview appointments, which were particularly challenging and messy. Participants often assumed that I would operate on "African time" and be more understanding compared to a strictly punctual Western individual. Some participants expressed, "She will understand; she is not a strict white person". While I empathised with their perspective, it became problematic when certain participants did not attend scheduled interviews and had to reschedule or arrived significantly late (1 to 2 hours after the scheduled time) or early, becoming frustrated when I was not present, prompting calls to inquire about my whereabouts. Those who arrived early without prior notice had often left by the time I arrived at the venue at previously agreed time. Consequently, some potential three participants were lost due to "African time", which was acceptable due to the flexibility inherent in a decolonial methodology. However, through follow-up efforts, patience, and understanding of the community's operating norms, it was possible to reschedule and eventually meet with some of them.

Gender-Based Boundaries

When conducting interviews with individuals from different genders and backgrounds, it is crucial to respect and adhere to cultural norms to prevent cultural confusion, misunderstandings, or conflicts. Age groups, as mentioned above, construct social relationships and the interactions between seniors and juniors, and gender differences, specifically in relation to the researcher, exemplify such norms. Additionally, it has been acknowledged that gender differences between the researcher and the participants play a significant role in conducting sensitive research involving vulnerable groups or exploring sensitive gendered experiences (Liamputtong & Ezzy, 2005). Prior to commencing this research, I had a good understanding of the gender differences within the South Sudanese community. Therefore, it was emphasised that this research aimed neither to shame men (a stigma many South Sudanese already feel) nor to assign blame or guilt but rather to explore experiences of family violence and intervention orders, as well as the cultural contributions to the prevention of family violence. This approach put both the participants and the researcher on the same level of willingness to discuss, listen, and learn from one another. All participants were encouraged to share their stories only when they felt convinced and comfortable to do so.

Research Design

This book draws on a qualitative dataset collected as part of the author's doctoral research project over three years, studying the experiences of family violence intervention orders and the role of culture in the South Sudanese community in Australia. A qualitative approach was chosen to allow data to emerge organically and provide an in-depth exploration of participants' experiences in resolving family violence intervention orders. This approach is particularly suitable when studying vulnerable groups, such as the participants in this research. In-depth interviews are effective in capturing the needs of vulnerable groups as they enable participants to actively engage in the research and share their stories. They foster a meaning-making partnership between the researcher and participant, requiring 'active asking and listening' to obtain information from the participant's perspective (Liamputtong, 2009).

The fieldwork for this research spanned eight months, from March to October 2022. During this period, I employed two strategies to recruit participants. Before entering the field, I identified relevant services and locations where a significant number of African individuals reside in Victoria. I then established contact with these identified services and leveraged my professional network to facilitate the dissemination of my recruitment materials. The endorsement and involvement of these services assured me that I was collaborating with influential and trustworthy figures who would be receptive to my research endeavours.

Ethical approval was sought and obtained through the La Trobe University Ethics Committee by submitting a detailed ethics application that addressed various aspects of the study, including the authenticity of gathered information and risk management strategies. Participant recruitment commenced only after receiving formal ethics approval from the La Trobe Human Research Ethics Committee.

I also engaged with South Sudanese community gatekeepers and respected leaders and elders. In this phase of recruitment, participants who heard about the research from community leaders were given the opportunity to ask questions and obtain more information before deciding whether to participate. To minimise coercion, leaders only distributed information about the research. It was left entirely to potential participants to contact me for further details. Those who expressed initial interest in the study—whether through FV and social support services or through community leaders, over the phone or in person—were given the chance to ask questions before the actual interview. During these preliminary meetings, I provided a detailed explanation of my research and ensured that participants fully understood their role should they choose to consent. This approach alleviated potential misunderstandings and enabled those who grasped the study's aims and potential benefits to share information within the community and identify individuals they believed would contribute meaningfully to the research. This facilitated a smooth recruitment process through snowball sampling.

Twenty South Sudanese individuals with experience of family violence intervention orders, either as applicants or as respondents, were interviewed. Each interview lasted between 60 and 90 minutes. At the start of each interview, participants were assured of the confidentiality of their responses and the de-identification of any identifiable information (Rubin & Rubin, 2012). To capture the interviews, I utilised a personal Olympus VN-541PC Voice Recorder with 16 GB of internal memory, providing ample recording capacity (Brown & Jones, 2016). Immediately after each interview, the recorded data was transferred to my secure university storage system (R: Drive/OneDrive) to prevent data loss and maintain confidentiality (Miles, 2015).

For data analysis, the study employed an inductive approach to allow the data to speak for itself without imposing pre-existing theories or concepts (Brewer, 2003). During the analysis phase, I utilised NVivo software to systematically organise and code the data thematically. As Creswell (2013, pp. 201–202) highlights, computer programs offer several advantages, including improved organisation and easy retrieval of research files, enhanced scrutiny of data, and the ability to map abstract concepts visually.

Sample Size

The in-depth semi-structured interviews involved twenty South Sudanese women and men, all of whom had firsthand experience with family violence intervention orders, either as applicants or as respondents. These individuals had recently experienced family violence and had either applied for or responded to a family violence intervention order in the state.

To ensure a balanced representation of perspectives, an equal number of male and female participants were sought. This gender balance aimed to reflect the diversity within the community and acknowledge that family violence affects individuals irrespective of gender. The size of the participant group was proportionate to the South Sudanese community in Australia, ensuring the findings remained relevant and representative.

Ethical Considerations and Risk Management

The study of violence is inherently sensitive, particularly for individuals who may have experienced prior trauma. For the participants in this research, previous experiences of violence during the war, along with the enduring hardships faced throughout the migration process and settlement in Australia, have contributed to complex trauma (Pease & Rees, 2006). Consequently, extensive discussions took place between my supervisors and me to determine the most appropriate approach for engaging with individuals and the community on this sensitive and often taboo subject. Participants were provided with information about La Trobe University counselling services and other community health services in case they needed support after the interviews.

Given the participants' backgrounds, it was crucial to consider and acknowledge potential ethical issues that could arise. Special attention was given to maintaining integrity in knowledge production and ensuring responsibility for the emotional, physical, and intellectual wellbeing of the participants throughout the entire research process, from pre-research planning to post-research follow-up.

Comprehensive measures were implemented to minimise both foreseeable and unforeseeable risks, ensuring the protection of both participants and the researcher. Ethical approval was sought and obtained from the La Trobe University Ethics Committee through a detailed ethics application that addressed various aspects of the study, including the authenticity of gathered information and risk management strategies. Participant recruitment commenced only after formal ethics approval was granted by the La Trobe Human Research Ethics Committee.

Reflexivity

Inevitably, social research is influenced and shaped by the socio-historical location and the researcher's biography, challenging their traditional beliefs and activist assumptions (Hammersley & Atkinson, 2019). Throughout all phases of this research, I prioritise the process of reflexivity. This involves recognising that both the researcher and the researched mutually and continuously influence each other.

In this case, my reflexivity includes reflecting on my perspective regarding South Sudanese experiences of violence, both historically and in the present, and acknowledging how pre-existing understandings of this issue are often reshaped in the light of new insights. This, in turn, affects my approach to the research. It is essential to describe the contextual relationships, such as my ethnic identity, in relation to the participants, as doing so enhances the credibility of the findings and deepens our understanding of the research.

Such a focus on self-awareness and sensitivity enables me to recognise the role of the self in the creation of knowledge, carefully self-monitoring the potential impact of my biases, and maintaining a balance between personal perspectives, community considerations, and universal insights. Practically, I remain mindful that researching family violence and intervention orders within the South Sudanese community, as part of the broader African Australian communities, presents significant challenges. As a fellow African Australian, this work requires a heightened level of self-consciousness and a willingness to step outside my comfort zone, embracing new perspectives on a system I once thought I fully understood.

Organisation of the Book

This book critically examines the ongoing efforts to decolonise legal systems response to FV in settler-colonial countries, particularly focusing on Australia. It explores the intersections of law, culture, migration, and family violence within the South Sudanese community. By engaging with decolonial theory, feminist scholarship, and Indigenous legal traditions, the book highlights the urgent need for culturally responsive legal interventions that acknowledge the historical and structural legacies of colonialism in the broader African Australian communities with particular focus on South Sudanese community.

This book is composed of nine chapters. Chapter 2 introduces the Australian migration system and explores African Australians' migration and settlement experiences. It examines how pre-migration factors, such as colonialism and war, disrupted peace processes and hindered social and economic development, ultimately shaping migration patterns for African Australians. The chapter contextualises the colonial legacies of violence. It discusses how these intersect with various forms of harm, including the effects of patriarchal gender norms, pre-migration trauma, systemic racism, and both gendered and racialised violence. These issues contribute to the challenges African Australians face during resettlement, including criminalisation and over-policing in contemporary Australia. Finally, the chapter highlights how these factors intersect with family and community dynamics, perpetuating experiences of family violence.

Chapter 3 presents empirical findings on the key factors driving family violence within the South Sudanese community. It examines how acculturation, gender roles, intergenerational trauma, displacement, and economic instability contribute to the persistence of family violence. The chapter also explores the impact of violence on individuals and families, community responses, and the tensions between traditional intervention methods and Australia's formal justice system response. By centring the voices of South Sudanese individuals, including applicants and respondents of Family Violence Intervention Orders (FVIOs), this chapter provides a nuanced understanding of the complex dynamics influencing family violence in the community, with significant implications for informing future interventions.

Chapter 4 explores African customary law practices in Africa concerning family matters, specifically focusing on family violence. Before and after colonisation, Africa maintained a pluralistic legal system that integrated statutory and customary law. In many African countries, customary law is recognised and enshrined in their constitutions, functioning similarly to family law in countries like Australia. Each

African country has its unique body of customary law that governs various aspects of family life, including resolving disputes such as family violence. Despite the diversity of these legal traditions, there are notable similarities across different regions, which reflect shared cultural values and practices. This chapter centres on how customary law is applied in addressing family disputes, particularly in the context of family violence. The discussion highlights how customary law has historically served as a cornerstone of social order in African communities, shedding light on its continued relevance and application today. Additionally, it examines how these customary practices intersect with statutory law, especially in post-colonial societies, and the implications this has for individuals and families facing legal challenges. The chapter concludes by summarising the arguments for and against using customary law in family violence matters and indicates which side this book supports.

Chapter 5 discusses how Australian family law functions—or fails to function—within the context of legal pluralism. It aims to assess whether the legal system accommodates the diverse needs of African Australians and other migrant communities while navigating the complexities of formal and African customary legal frameworks. Despite numerous amendments to the Family Law Act 1975, including recent changes that have recognised same-sex marriage, there has been limited focus on legal pluralism within Australia (Juuk, 2023). This includes a lack of attention to how refugee, migrant, and Indigenous communities engage with both formal and customary legal systems (Juuk, 2023). By examining these aspects, Chapter 5 aims to shed light on how effectively the Australian family law system addresses the needs of diverse social groups and identifies gaps where improvements are necessary. The chapter highlights how legal pluralism could be better integrated into the Australian legal framework to ensure that all communities, including African Australian communities, receive equitable and culturally sensitive legal support. Chapters 4 and 5 not only provide crucial background for the subsequent chapters, which present empirical analyses of the experiences of South Sudanese Australians but also stand as significant contribution.

Chapter 6 presents empirical findings regarding victims' perspectives on their interactions with law enforcement during incidents of family violence. This chapter examines how these perspectives challenge common assumptions about legal remedies and shed light on broader issues within the Australian policing system. The failure of the policing system, rooted in Australia's colonial history, to adequately serve diverse communities—particularly Indigenous peoples, migrants, and refugees—has been well-documented. This chapter argues that, given the complex colonial history of policing faced by migrant and refugee communities, such as the South Sudanese community, many victims often feel unsupported due to deep-seated fears and mistrust of the Australian police. By highlighting these challenges, Chapter 6 provides a more nuanced understanding of why some victims hesitate to engage with state systems and calls for the implementation of more culturally sensitive and effective support mechanisms.

Chapter 7 presents victims-survivors (applicants) experiences of FVIOs detailed narratives following incidents of family violence within the South Sudanese Australian community. The chapter highlights their experiences with the legal system, including their interactions with legal practitioners. The chapter offers insights into how individuals accessed these orders, the events during their enforcement, and their preferences for an ideal intervention process. Drawing from participants' experiences, it discusses the implementation of FVIOs, evaluates their effectiveness, and explores the consequences faced by applicants and respondents due to these orders. In addition, Chapter 8 expands on the relationship between cultural interventions within the community and formal legal interventions. The chapter scrutinises the procedural aspects of the FVIO system and how these affect individuals seeking and receiving justice. By examining these elements, Chapter 7 provides a comprehensive understanding of the strengths and weaknesses of the current intervention order system from the perspectives of those directly impacted by family violence.

Chapter 8 explores alternative approaches proposed by South Sudanese Australians to address family violence when FVIOs are inadequate in stopping violence within families and in intimate relationships in their community. Applicants and respondents have reported that relying solely on FVIOs often fails to prevent family violence effectively. In this chapter, I will discuss specific alternative strategies suggested by participants that could be used alongside or instead of FVIOs. These approaches aim to reduce reliance on FVIO applications and tackle the underlying issues within families and intimate partnerships. The chapter will examine these proposed methods, highlighting how they could offer more comprehensive solutions and potentially leading to more sustainable reductions in family violence. By incorporating these insights, the chapter seeks to enhance understanding of effective family violence intervention and prevention strategies tailored to the needs of the South Sudanese community, the broader African Australian communities and communities with similar backgrounds and experiences of FVIOs.

Chapter 9: this concluding chapter summarises the study's key findings and highlights the complexities of family violence within the South Sudanese Australian community and the broader African Australian experience. The chapter advocates for a decolonial approach to addressing family violence in communities affected by colonialism and its historical violence. It situates these experiences within historical and systemic contexts, recognising the lasting impacts of colonisation, war, displacement, trauma, and stressors related to migration. By examining how racial discrimination, economic marginalisation, and cultural disconnection influence experiences of violence and access to support services, this chapter emphasises the inadequacy of mainstream interventions that fail to address these intersecting factors. In doing so, it aims to contribute to ongoing discussions about decolonising responses to family violence and developing more inclusive and effective support systems for communities with complex histories of violence and marginalisation.

References

Abimbola, S. (2019). The foreign gaze: Authorship in academic global health, vol. 4, e002068. https://doi.org/10.1136/bmjgh-2019-002068.

Abur, W. (2023). Migration and settlement of African people in Australia. *IntechOpen.* https://doi.org/10.5772/intechopen.107083

Armytage P., Ogloff J. (2017). *Youth justice review and strategy meeting needs and reducing offending* (part 1–3). Department of Justice and Regulation. https://www.justice.vic.gov.au/justice-system/youth-justice/youth-justice-review-and-strategy-meeting-needs-and-reducing-offending

Atkinson, J. (2010). *Trauma trails, recreating song lines: The transgenerational effects of trauma in Indigenous Australia*. Spinifex Press.

Australian Bureau of Statistics. (2014). *4517.0—Prisoners in Australia*, 2014. http://www.abs.gov.au/ausstats/abs@.nsf/Lookup/by%20Subject/4517.0_2014_Main%20Features_Country%20of%20birth_7

Australian Bureau of Statistics. (2017). *Prisoners in Australia*, 2017. http://www.abs.gov.au/ausstats/abs@.nsf/Lookup/by%20Subject/4517.0~2017~Main%20Features~Country%20of%20birth~9

Betts, R. F. (2004). *Decolonization*. Routledge.

Bhargava, R. (2013). Overcoming the epistemic injustice of colonialism. *Global Policy, 4*, 413–417. https://doi.org/10.1111/1758-5899.12093

Bogdan, R. C., & Biklen, S. K. (1992). *Qualitative research for education: An introduction to theory and methods* (2nd ed.). Allyn and Bacon.

Boonzaier, F., & Van Niekerk, T. (2019). *Decolonial feminist community psychology*. Springer Nature.

Brewer, J. D. (2003). *Ethnography*. Open University Press.

Brown, H., & Jones, J. A. (2016). Immigrant rights are civil rights. *Contexts, 15*(2), 34–39. https://doi.org/10.1177/1536504216648149

Campbell, E., Bissett, T., Howard, A., Lewers, N., Polis, M., & Richter, J. (2021). *More than just a piece of paper: Getting protection orders made in a safe and supported way: Responding to Recommendation 77 of the Royal Commission into family violence* (pp. 1–130). RMIT University, Melbourne.

Collins, P. H. (1990). Black feminist thought: Knowledge, consciousness, and the politics of empowerment. Routledge.

Coventry, G., Dawes, G., Moston, S., & Palmer, D. (2015). *Sudanese Refugees' experiences with the Queensland criminal justice system*. CQUniversity. Report. https://hdl.handle.net/10018/1238523

Coventry, L., Guerra, C., MacKenzie, D., & Pinkney, S. (2014). Youth justice in Australia: Themes from recent inquiries. Australian Institute of Health and Welfare. https://www.aihw.gov.au/reports/youth-justice/youth-justice-inaustralia-themes-from-recent-inquiries

Craib, R. B. (2017). Cartography and decolonization. In J. R. Akerman (Ed.), *Decolonizing the map: Cartography from colony to nation* (pp. 11–71). University of Chicago Press.

Creswell, J. W. (2013). *Qualitative inquiry & research design: Choosing among five approaches* (3rd ed.). SAGE Publications.

Department of Premier and Cabinet. (2018a). Family violence reform implementation monitor: Report of operations 1 November 2016 to 1 November 2017. Victorian Government. https://www.vic.gov.au/family-violence-reform

Dickson-Swift, V., James, E. L., Kippen, S., & Liamputtong, P. (2007). Doing sensitive research: What challenges do qualitative researchers face? *Qualitative Research, 7*(3), 327–353. https://doi.org/10.1177/1468794107078515

Dudley, M. (2006). Mental health and cultural competence in refugee populations. In P. Allotey (Ed.), The health of refugees: Public health perspectives from crisis to settlement (pp. 90–108). Oxford University Press.

Fanon, F. (1963). *The wretched of the earth.* Grove Press.

Fisher, C. (2013). Changed and changing gender and family roles and domestic violence in African refugee background communities post-settlement in Perth, Australia. *Violence against Women, 19*(7), 833–847. https://doi.org/10.1177/1077801213497535

Fitz-Gibbon, K., & Walklate, S. (2023). *What is to be done about violence against women?* Taylor & Francis.

Forson, M. (2019). *The experiences of African Victorian young people. Findings and recommendations report*. African Australian Community Taskforce.

Gabbidon, S. (2010). Introduction. In S. Gabbidon (Ed.), Race, *ethnicity, crime, and justice: An international Dilemma* (pp. 1–15). SAGE.

Glenn, E. N. (2015). Settler colonialism as structure: A framework for comparative studies of US race and gender formation. *Sociology of Race and Ethnicity, 1*, 52–72. https:// doi.org/https://doi.org/10.1177/2332649214560440.

Hammersley, M., & Atkinson, P. (2019). *Ethnography: Principles in practice* (4th ed.). Routledge. https://doi.org/10.4324/9781315146027

Hardin, M. (2002). Altering masculinities: The Spanish conquest and the evolution of the Latin American machismo. *International Journal of Sexuality and Gender Studies, 7*, 1–22. https://doi.org/10.1023/A:1013050829597

James, P. B., Renzaho, A. M. N., Mwanri, L., Miller, I., Wardle, J., Gatwiri, K., & Lauche, R. (2022). The prevalence of anxiety, depression, and post-traumatic stress disorder among African migrants: A systematic review and meta-analysis. *Psychiatry Research, 317*, Article 114899. https://doi.org/10.1016/j.psychres.2022.114899

Juuk, B. G. A. (2023). *Family dispute resolution from a cultural perspective.* Cambridge Scholars Publishing.

Khan, M., Abimbola, S., Aloudat, T., Capobianco, E., Hawkes, S., & Rahman-Shepherd, A. (2021). Decolonising global health in 2021: A roadmap to move from rhetoric to reform. *BMJ Global Health, 6*, Article e005604. https://doi.org/10.1136/bmjgh-2021-005604

Krugman, D. W. (2023). Global health and the elite capture of decolonization: On reformism and the possibilities of alternate paths. *PLOS Global Public Health, 3*, Article e0002103. https://doi.org/10.1371/journal.pgph.0002103

Laviosa, S., Pagano, A., Kemppanen, H., & Ji, M. (2017). *Textual and contextual analysis in empirical translation studies.* Singapore Springer Singapore.

Liamputtong, P., & Ezzy, D. (2005). *Qualitative research methods.* Oxford University Press.

Liamputtong, P. (2010). *Performing qualitative cross-cultural research.* Cambridge University Press.

Mannell, J., Hawkes, S., & Pallitto, C. (2021). Intimate partner violence and women's physical and mental health in low-and middle-income countries: A systematic review of longitudinal studies. *PLOS ONE, 16*(3), e0247055. https://doi.org/10.1371/journal.pone.0247055

Marlowe, J. (2012). 'They have already thrown away their culture': South Sudanese refugee perceptions of integration in Australia. *Journal of Intercultural Studies, 33*(5), 529–547. https://doi.org/10.1080/07256868.2012.701440

Maschke, K. J. (1997). *The legal response to violence against women.* Garland.

Mclean, S. (2005). *The basics of interpersonal communication.* Pearson.

Miles, M. B. (2015). *Qualitative data analysis + the coding manual for qualitative researchers* (3rd ed.). Sage Publications.

Milos, D. (2011). *South Sudanese communities and Australian family law: A clash of systems. The Australasian Review of African Studies, 32*(2), 143–159. https://search.informit.org/doi/https://doi.org/10.3316/informit.522836468928978

Mungai, N. W., & Gitau, L. W. (2019). African refugee women in Australia: Domestic and family violence experience. In A. Kalunta-Crumpton (Ed.), *Violence against women of African descent: Global perspectives* (1st ed., pp. 211–228). Lexington Books.

Naicker, V. (2023). The problem of epistemological critique in contemporary Decolonial theory. *Social Dynamics, 49*, 220–241. https://doi.org/10.1080/02533952.2023.2226497

Pease, B., & Rees, S. (2006). Theorising men's violence towards women in refuges: Making sense of competing masculinities in a context of trauma. In B. Pease & M. Pringle (Eds.), Critical perspectives on masculinity and violence (pp. 100–116). Routledge.

Peace Direct. (2021). Time to decolonise aid: Insights and lessons from a global consultation. *London, UK: Adesco, Alliance for Peacebuilding, Peace Direct, WCAPS, Women of Color Advancing Peace, Security and Conflict Transformation.*

Pernice, R. (1994). Methodological issues in research with refugees and immigrants. *Professional Psychology: Research and Practice, 25*(3), 207–213. https://doi.org/10.1037/0735-7028.25.3.207

Pittaway, T., Riggs, E., & Dantas, J. A. R. (2022). Intergenerational conflict among resettled South Sudanese in Australia. *Transcultural psychiatry*, 13634615221105115. Advance online publication. https://doi.org/10.1177/13634615221105115

Quijano, A. (2000). Coloniality of power and eurocentrism in Latin America. *International Sociology, 15*, 215–232. https://doi.org/10.1177/026858090001500200

Reeves, E. (2020). Family violence, protection orders and systems abuse: Views of legal practitioners. *Current Issues in Criminal Justice, 32*(1), 91–110. https://doi.org/10.1080/10345329.2019.1665816

Reeves, E. (2021). I'm not at all protected and I think other women should know that, that they're not protected either': Victim–Survivors' experiences of 'Misidentification' in Victoria's family violence system". *International Journal for Crime, Justice and Social Democracy, 10*(4), 39–51. https://doi.org/10.5204/ijcjsd.1992

Robinson, K., Afrouz, R., & Dunwoodie, K. (2025). Domestic and family violence among migrant, refugee, and asylum-seeking women in Australia: A scoping review of experiences and support. *Journal of Family Violence.* https://doi.org/10.1007/s10896-025-00823-2

Rubin, H., & Rubin, I. (2012). Qualitative interviewing: The art of hearing data (3rd ed.). Sage.

Sahib, H., Hanafiah, W., Aswad, M., Yassi, A., & Mashhadi, F. (2021). Syntactic configuration of code-switching between Indonesian and English: Another perspective on code-switching Phenomena. *Education Research International, 2021*, 1–10. https://doi.org/10.1155/2021/3402485

Said, E. W. (1995). Orientalism (Reprinted ed.). Penguin Books. (Original work published 1978)

Segrave, M., Wilson, D., & Fitz-Gibbon, K. (2016). Policing intimate partner violence in Victoria (Australia): Examining police attitudes and the potential of specialisation. *Australian & New Zealand Journal of Criminology, 51*(1), 99–116. https://doi.org/10.1177/0004865816679686(Originalwork published2018)

Shay, O. (2015). To switch or not to switch: Code-switching in a multilingual country. *Procedia—Social and Behavioral Sciences, 209*, 462–469. https://doi.org/10.1016/j.sbspro.2015.11.253.

Shepherd, S. M., Newton, D., & Farquharson, K. (2018). Pathways to offending for young Sudanese Australians. *Australian and New Zealand Journal of Criminology, 51*(4), 481–501. https://doi.org/10.1177/000486581774926

Shepherd, S. M., & Spivak, B. L. (2020). Estimating the extent and nature of offending by Sudanese-born individuals in Victoria. *Australian and New Zealand Journal of Criminology, 53*(3), 352–368. https://doi.org/10.1177/0004865820929066

Shohat, E. (1992). Notes on the" post-colonial". *Social Text* 99–113.

Singh, N. S., Lokot, M., Undie, C.-C., Onyango, M. A., Morgan, R., Harmer, A., et al. (2021). Research in forced displacement: Guidance for a feminist and decolonial approach. *Lancet, 397*, 560–562. https://doi.org/10.1016/S0140-6736(21)00024-6

Smith, L. T. (2022). *Decolonizing methodologies: Research and indigenous peoples.* Zed Books Ltd.

Smith, L. T. (1999). *Decolonizing methodologies: Research and indigenous peoples.* Bloomsbury Publishing.

Tarpey-Brown, G., Kirwan, J., Wise, S., Alisic, E., Vaughan, C., & Block, K. (2024). Domestic and family violence affecting children and young people from culturally and racially marginalized migrant backgrounds in Australia: A scoping review of child experiences and service responses. *Trauma, Violence & Abuse, 25*(5), 3872–3886. https://doi.org/10.1177/15248380241265386

Thambinathan, V., Kinsella, E. A. (2021). Decolonizing methodologies in qualitative research: Creating spaces for transformative praxis. *International Journal of Qualitative Methods, 20*. https://doi.org/10.1177/16094069211014766.

van der Kolk, B. (2014). *The body keeps the score: Brain, mind and body in the healing of trauma.* Penguin Books.

Walklate, S., Fitz-Gibbon, K., & McCulloch, J. (2017). Is more law the answer? Seeking justice for victims of intimate partner violence through the reform of legal categories. *Criminology & Criminal Justice, 18*(1), 115–131. https://doi.org/10.1177/1748895817728561(Originalworkpublished2018)

Warikandwa, T. V., Nhemachena, A., & Mpofu, N. (2017). Double victimisation? Law, decoloniality and research ethics in post-colonial Africa. *The Journal of Pan-African Studies, 10*(2), 64.

Zakumumpa, H., Diop, N., & Alhassan, R. K. (2023). Decolonizing global health: An agenda for research. *BMC Health Services Research, 23*, 832. https://doi.org/10.1186/s12913-023-09834-5

2

African Australian Migration and Settlement in Australia: Contextualising Histories of Violence and Legal Consciousness

Introduction

The chapter is divided into three parts. The first part provides a brief overview of the Australian migration system, including its developments over the years and the migration experiences, settlement processes, and contributions of African Australians to society. The second part examines the experiences of violence that African Australians face both before and after migrating, with a specific focus on how these experiences intersect with family violence. In the third part, I discuss the importance of understanding legal consciousness in shaping African Australians' responses to these intersections of violence.

Australian Immigration Policy

Waves of colonial expansion, government policies, and global socio-political changes have shaped Australia's migration history. Before British colonisation began in 1788, the continent was inhabited by First Nations peoples, who had lived on the land for over 65,000 years (Chingaipe,

A. K. Anyieth, *Decolonising Family Violence Legal Intervention Orders in African-Australian Communities*, https://doi.org/10.1007/978-3-031-95404-7_2

2024). These communities maintained rich cultural traditions, governance systems, and trade networks. The arrival of British settlers led to the forced displacement and violence against Indigenous communities, marking the beginning of Australia's identity as a settler-colonial nation (Colic-Peisker & Tilbury, 2007).

Australian migration predominantly comprised British and European settlers during the nineteenth and early twentieth centuries (Chingaipe, 2024). This was encouraged through various means, including convict transportation (1788–1868), the gold rush in the 1850s, and post-war resettlement programs. The White Australia Policy (1901–1973) imposed restrictions on non-European immigration, reinforcing racial exclusion (Chingaipe, 2024). However, the end of this policy in the 1970s initiated a shift towards multiculturalism, which opened Australia's borders to migrants and refugees from Asia, the Middle East, and Africa.

Migration of Africans to Australia

African migration to Australia has evolved and has been shaped by global events, Australian immigration policies, and humanitarian needs. Although African Australians remain a relatively small percentage of the population, migration from Africa has increased significantly since the late twentieth century. Today, Australia is recognised as one of the most culturally diverse nations in the world. Migration is now primarily driven by skilled labour programs, humanitarian resettlement, and family reunification (Colic-Peisker & Tilbury, 2007). Initially, African migrants arrived in Australia as former slaves from America and as convicts from Britain (Chingaipe, 2024), while more recent arrivals have come as refugees or asylum seekers. This historical migration pattern sets the stage for the challenges African migrants face in settling in Australia today (Abur, 2018; Colic-Peisker & Tilbury, 2007). Since the 1990s, there has been an increase in migration from Africa, including communities from South Sudan, Somalia, Ethiopia, and the Democratic Republic of Congo. Many of these individuals arrived as refugees fleeing conflict and political instability.

In the 2020 census, over 400,000 people living in Australia identified as being of African origin, representing 1.6% of the Australian population and 5.1% of Australia's overseas-born population. The majority (58%) were white South Africans, while 42% were black Africans from sub-Saharan countries (Australian Bureau of Statistics, 2019–20; Abur and Mphande, 2019). Most black Africans from sub-Saharan countries migrated either on humanitarian visas as refugees forcibly displaced by war, persecution, or other unprecedented circumstances in their home countries, or through skilled migration in search of better opportunities (Abur and Mphande, 2019). However, settlement for this cohort, particularly black Africans, has been challenging for many individuals and families due to several factors, including racism, interpersonal and systemic discrimination, unemployment, language barriers, and contradictions between traditions, cultural practices, and beliefs.

African Australians Contribution to Australian Society

Notwithstanding the negative reports, African Australians have significantly enriched Australia's cultural, social, economic, and political landscape. Their diverse backgrounds, with a rich tapestry of traditions, languages, and perspectives, have enhanced and deepened the Australian identity (Jakubowicz, 2018; Udah, 2019).

African Australians have made substantial contributions to the arts, music, business, and literature. Artists, musicians, and authors of African heritage have introduced unique narratives and styles, fostering a greater understanding and appreciation of African cultures within the broader Australian community (Tilbury, 2007). Many African Australians actively participate in community organisations and initiatives addressing social justice, education, and community cohesion (Pittaway & Muli, 2009). They serve as leaders and role models, advocating for their communities and promoting multiculturalism (Udah, 2019).

Economically, African Australians contribute through entrepreneurship, innovation, and workforce participation. Many bring valuable skills and diverse experiences that drive business growth and enhance economic diversity across various industries (Colic-Peisker & Tilbury, 2008). Additionally, African Australians have become increasingly engaged in political processes, advocating for the rights and interests of their communities. Their involvement in public discourse has helped raise awareness of issues such as racism, inequality, and immigration (Jakubowicz, 2018).

In sports, African Australians have made significant contributions, enhancing Australia's reputation in international competitions. Athletes of African heritage have become role models for younger generations and have had a profound influence on Australia's sporting culture (Duncan, 2016). As the African Australian population continues to grow, their contributions remain vital in shaping a more inclusive and diverse nation, reflecting Australia's strength in multiculturalism.

Pre-colonisation Africa

Before colonisation and internal conflicts, African societies maintained peace through customary laws at the family, clan, and tribal levels, believing that stability within these units ensured national harmony (Fadlalla Ali, 2009; Jok, 2011). Prior to the imposition of Common Law by colonial powers, African communities had well-established conflict resolution mechanisms rooted in customary governance (Jok, 2011). These laws regulated disputes, marriage, cohabitation, and family matters, reflecting Indigenous interpretations of justice. However, colonial authorities dismissed these systems as "informal" because they did not conform to Western legal structures.

To exert control, colonial administrations introduced the Chiefs Courts Ordinance, establishing customary courts led by appointed chiefs who were granted executive powers (Sachs, 2013). However, this system of indirect rule altered pre-existing legal frameworks, imposing standardised governance across diverse ethnic groups to serve colonial interests (Massoud, 2013). Traditional dispute resolution mechanisms—such as elder councils and kingdom-based adjudication—were replaced by colonial hierarchies of headmen, chiefs, and paramount chiefs (Higgins,

2011). This restructuring disrupted political orders, economic systems, and cultural identities (Johnson, 2011).

However, it is important to recognise that contemporary Africa and its people are not homogeneous. Africa is an immensely diverse continent comprising 54 nations, each with distinct cultural, linguistic, and historical identities (Falola, 2020). This diversity is celebrated by Africans both on the continent and in the diaspora, with each country preserving its rich traditions while evolving under the influence of globalisation, technology, and social movements (Nyamnjoh, 2017). A nuanced understanding of these differences fosters greater appreciation and respect for the multifaceted identities of African people.

Nonetheless, the shared history of colonial violence remains a fundamental part of Africa's narrative. Across generations, Africans continue to relive, reflect on, and articulate these experiences, deepening the understanding of the past and its lasting implications (Mamdani, 1996). Colonialism's legacy is complex, leaving enduring imprints on Africa's social, political, and economic landscapes. These legacies have played a significant role in driving mass migration from Africa to Western countries (Mbembe, 2001; Rodney, 1972). The colonial era was marked by severe brutality, oppression, and exploitation, leaving deep scars that persist today.

Systematic acts of colonial violence—including genocide, crimes against humanity (such as apartheid and slavery), and war crimes—continue to shape African societies (Cooper, 2002; Ndlovu-Gatsheni, 2013). European colonial powers—including the British, French, Portuguese, Germans, Spanish, and Belgians—imposed regimes of subjugation, exploitation, discrimination, disempowerment, and expropriation (Achebe, 1984; Fanon, 1963). These injustices have been compounded by contemporary global neoliberalism and ongoing forms of neo-colonialism, which continue to influence Africa's socioeconomic and political systems (Amin, 1972).

Moreover, many modern conflicts in African nations can be traced back to colonial constructs of ethnic identity, land distribution policies, and historical systems of exploitation and extraction, including slavery (Mamdani, 2001). Structural violence stemming from colonial histories continues to shape contemporary injustices, influencing both state policies and social relations. The lingering aftershocks of colonial violence remain deeply embedded in affected societies, impacting justice mechanisms and global perceptions of Africa (Mbembe, 2017).

Post-colonialism Conflicts and the Struggles for Resolutions

Violence in Africa did not end after independence but persisted into the post-colonial era. Scholars highlight that Africa continues to bear the psychological and structural impacts of colonial violence (Fanon, 1963). Fanon argued that oppressed people, having been subjected to violent domination, often adopt similar methods in their struggle for liberation. While some interpret his work as endorsing violence, Fanon was diagnosing its psychological roots, noting that both oppressors and the oppressed exhibited symptoms of mental distress. His experiences treating both torture victims and torturers revealed cycles of violence, including family violence, which continue today (Fanon, 1963). He urged the colonised to avoid emulating Europe, which professed human rights while committing atrocities globally.

Post-colonial Africa witnessed genocidal conflicts fuelled by internal divisions and Western-supplied arms (Achebe, 2012; Ekwe-Ekwe, 2006). Civil wars in Rwanda, Sudan, Congo, Liberia, Sierra Leone, Somalia, and Nigeria's war against the Igbo mirrored the colonial strategy of divide and rule. Similar patterns of violence appear in gang conflicts in North and South America, the Caribbean, and the Middle East, often involving African-descended populations (Durán & Campos, 2019). Some of these wars, such as Sudan's North–South conflict, lasted over two decades, leaving lasting instability beyond the colonial period.

African Australians Experiences of Violence

In Australia, African Australian communities have experienced and continue to experience various forms of violence both pre—and post-migration (Colic-Peisker & Tilbury, 2008; Udah, 2019). Their encounters with different systems during transitions and displacement—whether in refugee camps (for those who migrated as refugees) or throughout the broader migration process—have significantly created a continuum of oppression and trauma, reinforcing new categories of suffering post-settlement. Recognising this continuum is essential, as it highlights how different forms of oppression reinforce one another.

Understanding family violence within African Australian communities requires a holistic framework that acknowledges the interconnected forms of violence shaping their everyday lives. Crenshaw (1989) introduced intersectionality to explain how overlapping social identities—such as race, gender, class, and migration status—produce unique experiences of oppression. In the African Australian context, family violence cannot be separated from colonial, structural, cultural, and systemic violence. Addressing family violence requires a comprehensive approach that considers racial, cultural, economic, and legal inequalities (Crenshaw, 1989; Nair & Vollhardt, 2020). An intersectional gender framework, in this sense, recognises how different aspects of African Australian identity—race, culture, migration background, and socioeconomic status—interact with Australian legal interventions and family violence responses. These intersections shape the barriers that African Australians face and the consequences they experience.

African Australians hold a marginalised social position in Australian society, facing racial discrimination, economic exclusion, and social stigmatisation (Molla, 2021). Intersectionality serves as a valuable tool in understanding how these overlapping oppressions influence experiences of family violence. Family violence must be contextualised within broader socio-political and historical realities, including colonial legacies, capitalism, migration, and systemic racism.

Cultural Dislocation and Kinship Networks

In African communities, migration disrupts traditional family structures, weakening intergenerational relationships and increasing vulnerability to family violence. This cultural dislocation necessitates interventions that incorporate culturally relevant support systems (Mungai & Pease, 2009). The erosion of traditional kinship networks can lead to social isolation, reducing access to informal support systems that might otherwise help prevent or mitigate family violence.

Patriarchal Gender Norms

Family violence in African Australian communities arises from the complex interplay of patriarchy, culture, negative masculine constructs, and external forms of violence projected onto the community and its people (Muchoki, 2013). Patriarchal cultural beliefs and traditions that emphasise male dominance and assertiveness shape constructions of masculinity and reinforce family violence (Muchoki, 2013). The relationship between culture, masculinity, and family violence in African Australian communities significantly influences how these experiences unfold (Kuyini et al., 2022).

Patriarchal structures are deeply embedded in traditional African contexts, shaping how many African Australian men construct and perform their masculinity and the meanings they attach to it (Muchoki, 2013). Gender hierarchies and rigid notions of masculine and feminine roles, which remain prevalent in many African Australian cultures, have profound implications for family violence (Muchoki, 2013). The enforcement of strict gender roles through cultural expectations and the dominant position of men within households contributes to these experiences (Muchoki, 2013). Nevertheless, addressing family violence in African Australian communities requires a comprehensive approach that not only challenges patriarchal cultural norms and harmful expressions of masculinity but also acknowledges the broader forms of violence and oppression these communities face.

Systemic Racism and Social Exclusion

African Australians frequently experience racial profiling, employment discrimination, and negative media portrayals, all of which contribute to social exclusion and increased family tensions (Farquharson & Nolan, 2018; Nunn, 2010). These racialised experiences create an environment where external stressors—such as economic disadvantage and social marginalisation—can exacerbate family violence (Muchoki, 2013). The internalisation of these racialised experiences also influences family dynamics, often leading to intergenerational tension and conflict (Udah, 2023).

In Australia, these challenges are deeply rooted in enduring anti-Black sentiment, which has shaped national ideologies since the country's colonial inception. Australia was established as an "isolated outpost of white supremacy" by British colonisers in the 1770s (Foley, 2011: p 609). Anti-Black and anti-Blak racism is well-documented within Australia's violent colonial history and its ongoing legacy of white possession, domination, and systemic exclusion of First Nations peoples (Udah, 2023). This deep-seated racial hierarchy is further reflected in Australia's early immigration policies, such as the Immigration Restriction Act of 1901, which sought to maintain a racially homogeneous society (Udah, 2023).

Criminalisation and Over-Policing

African Australian men and youth face disproportionate policing, high incarceration rates, and increased criminalisation (Hunter, 2018). This over-surveillance fosters distrust in legal systems, discouraging families from seeking assistance in cases of family violence. African Australians have reported elevated levels of perceived discrimination and racial profiling, contributing to feelings of social and economic exclusion (Benier et al., 2018; Forson, 2019; Markus, 2016; Weber, 2018).

Media coverage of African Australians' involvement in criminal activities has heightened anxieties within segments of the community, particularly among the South Sudanese population (Benier et al., 2018; Forson, 2019; Henriques-Gomes, 2018). A well-publicised series of offences committed by a small number of predominantly South Sudanese youth in Victoria between 2016 and 2018 sparked contentious and reactionary local and national debates (Watkins & Sood, 2017). These discussions centred on the extent of African Australians' involvement in specific violent crimes, the desirability of increasing refugee intake from Africa, and the role of anti-African sentiment in criminal profiling (see Majavu, 2020; Shepherd & Spivak, 2020). The criminalisation of African Australian communities contributes to family instability, as affected individuals often face prolonged separation from their families due to incarceration, exacerbating economic and emotional hardships (Udah, 2023).

Everyday Violence and Its Impact on Family Dynamics

Scheper-Hughes and Bourgois (2004) conceptualise everyday violence as the normalised harm resulting from systemic inequality. African Australians experience multiple forms of everyday violence that contribute to family violence, including socioeconomic disadvantage, racial discrimination, and legal marginalisation (Udah, 2023). These intersecting forms of violence create an environment in which African Australian families may struggle to access the resources and support systems needed to mitigate family violence.

Economic Marginalisation

In addition, African Australians experience higher rates of unemployment, underemployment, and housing insecurity (Abur, 2016). Economic hardship exacerbates family tensions, while financial instability limits survivors' ability to leave abusive situations (Colic-Peisker & Tilbury, 2007). Economic precarity also restricts access to essential services such as legal aid, counselling, and crisis housing, further entrenching cycles of violence, dependence, and marginalisation.

Interconnectedness of Violence

It is essential to understand that these forms of violence are interconnected and reinforce each other. Everyday experiences of violence within African Australian communities cause profound harm, affecting individuals, families, and the broader community in multiple ways (Udah, 2023). The emotional and psychological toll can manifest as chronic stress, anxiety, depression, and post-traumatic stress disorder (PTSD), particularly for those who experience ongoing or intergenerational trauma (Majavu, 2020). This distress can impact a person's sense of self-worth, relationships, and ability to engage in daily life, reinforcing cycles of violence and social disconnection (Majavu, 2020).

The physical consequences of violence range from injuries to long-term health complications, including disability and, in extreme cases, death (African Think Tank, 2019). Survivors often experience lasting medical issues, while fear of violence may restrict their freedom of movement and access to essential services such as healthcare, education, and employment (Udah, 2023). These limitations not only affect individuals but also have broader socioeconomic repercussions, weakening community resilience, and perpetuating disadvantage (Abdelkerim & Grace, 2012; African Think Tank, 2019).

Furthermore, violence disrupts family dynamics and stability, creating divisions within households and undermining traditional support structures. Children exposed to violence are particularly vulnerable, as they may struggle with developmental, behavioural, and emotional challenges that impact their future relationships and social integration (Cohealth, 2018). The erosion of trust within families and communities contributes to ongoing cycles of violence, making it difficult to navigate other aspects of life. Addressing everyday violence requires culturally responsive interventions that prioritise healing, accountability, and structural change to ensure safety and well-being for all.

An intersectional lens (Intersections of Violence in African Australian Communities, n.d.) helps to understand how various aspects of identity—such as race, gender, and class—intersect to shape experiences of violence and marginalisation.

African Australian Legal Consciousness

The experiences of multiple forms of violence pre—and post-settlement in the African Australian communities influence their legal consciousness, particularly how they see themselves before the law (Pittaway & Muli, 2009). Legal consciousness refers to how individuals perceive and interact with the law, encompassing both explicit and implicit understandings of legal norms and institutions (Horák, Lacko, & Klocek, 2021). Although legal rules may not always directly influence people's daily decisions, intimate and family disputes often intersect with legal matters (Nielsen & Nieson, 2005). Nielsen (2005) argues that legal consciousness shapes how individuals interpret interactions, identify problematic situations, and perceive possible remedies or responses (Westoby, 2008). It also includes assumptions about the law individuals take for granted (Westoby, 2008).

The legal consciousness of African Australians is shaped by historical and contemporary factors, including the colonial imposition of legal structures that competed with Indigenous customary law (Buol, 2023). Forced migration, experiences in refugee camps, and transition processes significantly influence their legal perceptions (Buol, 2023). Furthermore, Australian migration and refugee policies, as well as the ambiguous legal status of some African migrants, contribute to their complex relationship with the law.

Adopting a decolonial perspective is essential for understanding how family issues, including family violence, were traditionally resolved in African societies (excluding white South African and white Zimbabwean populations). Traditional dispute resolution mechanisms, alongside encounters with multiple legal systems, shape how African Australians engage with Australian law (Buol, 2023). Their interactions with legal institutions are influenced by past experiences and cultural norms, which in turn shape their legal consciousness (Buol, 2023).

Legal consciousness research provides a framework for analysing how individuals navigate legal challenges, emphasising subjective legal experiences over broader societal impacts (Silbey, 2005). Ethnographic studies show that people interpret legal events within cultural norms and moral frameworks, shaping their perceptions of wrongdoing and justice (Silbey, 2005). Benda-Beckmann and Turner (2019) highlight that migrants bring legal customs, including religious and national laws, which often conflict with host country laws, creating challenges for both legal institutions and migrant communities. In Victoria, for example, media portrayals have contributed to negative perceptions of African Australians, labelling young people as "lawless thugs" (Panahi, 2016, p.1).

Ewick and Silbey (1998, 2009) categorise legal consciousness into three paradigms: before the law, with the law, and against the law (Silbey, 2005). Individuals before the law view it as a formal, hierarchical system separate from daily life, reflecting dominant Western legal structures in Australia. Those with the law see it as a flexible set of rules that can be strategically used, while those against the law perceive it as oppressive and resist its authority (Silbey, 2005). These perspectives shape individuals' legal engagement: for instance, those with the law are more likely to seek legal assistance, whereas those before or against the law may feel alienated from legal institutions. For instance, in the context of family violence, help-seeking during a family violence incident might depend on individuals' legal consciousness. Victims' willingness to seek legal support, including police intervention, is shaped by past experiences with law enforcement both in Australia and their countries of origin. In conflict-affected regions such as South Sudan, the Democratic Republic of Congo, Somalia, parts of Ethiopia, Eritrea, and north-eastern Nigeria, legal systems often collapse, leading to irregular legal practices and a loss of public trust in justice institutions (Aduot, 2021). As a result, law enforcement may be viewed with suspicion rather than as a means of justice (Benda-Beckmann & Turner, 2019). These experiences shape African Australians' perceptions of the law and influence their legal consciousness in Australia.

Conclusion

In this chapter, I provide a concise history of Australian migration, including its origins and the advancements made in migration policy. This discussion highlights the changes that have allowed migrants from countries other than Britain to settle in Australia. Additionally, the chapter explores the migration of African Australians to Australia, examining their colonial histories and experiences in settler-colonial Australia.

In conclusion, the settlement experiences of African Australians, particularly those from refugee and humanitarian backgrounds, have been shaped by systemic and interpersonal challenges, as well as settler-colonial legacies such as racism, discrimination, and socioeconomic barriers. These challenges, combined with pre-existing legal traditions and customary dispute resolution practices, influence how African Australians perceive justice, authority, and their place within Australian society. While some regard the legal system as a means of protection and redress, others view it as an extension of the colonial and structural inequalities they have historically faced.

This chapter argues that the various forms of violence intersecting within African Australian communities' shape and sometimes exacerbate their experiences of family violence, help-seeking behaviours, and access to legal support. Furthermore, while family violence is rooted in patriarchy and disproportionately affects individuals along gendered lines, African Australians' broader experiences of intersecting violence provide a contextual lens that captures the full scope of the disadvantages they encounter in Australia.

African Australians' legal consciousness is profoundly shaped by their historical experiences, migration journeys, and interactions with legal systems in their countries of origin and Australia. The legacy of colonial legal impositions forced migration and resettlement challenges has influenced how they perceive and engage with the law. As outlined in this chapter, legal consciousness extends beyond formal laws to include the ways in which individuals internalise, interpret, and respond to legal norms and institutions.

References

Abdelkerim, A. A., & Grace, M. (2012). Challenges to employment in newly emerging African communities in Australia: A review of the literature. *Australian Social Work, 65*(1), 104–119. https://doi.org/10.1080/0312407X.2011.616958

Abur, W. (2016). *Settlement strategies for the South Sudanese community in Australia: Social capital and the social fabric*. Scholars' Press.

Abur, W. (2018). *Settlement strategies for the South Sudanese Community in Melbourne: An analysis of employment and sport participation.* Melbourne: Victoria University. Available at: vuir.vu.edu.au/36189/

Abur, W., & Mphande, C. (2019). Mental Health and Wellbeing of South Sudanese-Australians. *Journal of Asian and African Studies, 55*(3), 412–428. https://doi.org/10.1177/0021909619880294 (Original work published 2020)

Abur, W. (2022). Migration and settlement of African people in Australia. In I. Muenstermann (Ed.), *Human migration in the last three centuries* (1st ed.). IntechOpen. https://doi.org/10.5772/intechopen.107083

Achebe, C. (1984). *The trouble with Nigeria.* Heinemann.

Achebe, C. (2012). *There was a country: A personal history of Biafra.* Penguin.

Aduot, D. (2021). The impact of civil conflict on legal institutions in Africa. *African Journal of Law and Society, 12*(3), 45–62.

African Think Tank. (2019). *African Australians settlement and integration 2030* [Conference session]. Opportunities and Challenges Conference 2018, Melbourne, Australia.

Amin, S. (1972). *Neo-colonialism in West Africa.* Monthly Review Press.

Australian Bureau of Statistics. (2019–20). *Migration, Australia.* ABS. https://www.abs.gov.au/statistics/people/population/migration-australia/latest-release.

Benda-Beckmann, K., & Turner, B. (2019). *Legal pluralism and migration: Conflicts between national and transnational laws.* Cambridge University Press.

Benier K., Blaustein J., Johns D., Maher S. (2018). *'Don't drag me into this': Growing up South Sudanese in Victoria after the 2016 Moomba 'riot'* (Full report). Centre for Multicultural Youth.

Buol, G. A. J. (2023). *Family dispute resolution from a cultural perspective.* Cambridge Scholars Publishing.

Chingaipe, S. (2024). *Black convicts: How slavery shaped Australia*. Pymble, NSW: Simon & Schuster Australia.
Cohealth. (2018). *Improving outcomes with South Sudanese Australians: A co-design project to build on community strengths and initiate new solutions*. https://www.cohealth.org.au/wp-content/uploads/2018/11/Improving-Outcomes-with-South-Sudanese-Australians.pdf
Colic-Peisker, V., & Tilbury, F. (2007). Integration into the Australian labour market: The experience of three "visibly different" groups of recently arrived refugees. *International Migration, 45*(1), 59–85. https://doi.org/10.1111/j.1468-2435.2007.00396.x
Colic-Peisker, V., & Tilbury, F. (2008). Being black in Australia: A case study of intergroup relations. *Journal of Intercultural Studies, 29*(4), 373–395. https://doi.org/10.1080/07256860802372268
Cooper, F. (2002). *Africa since 1940: The past of the present*. Cambridge University Press.
Crenshaw, K. (1989). Demarginalizing the intersection of race and sex: A Black feminist critique of antidiscrimination doctrine, feminist theory and antiracist politics. *University of Chicago Legal Forum, 1989*(1), 139–167.
Duncan, R. (2016). African Australians in sport: A study of integration and representation. *Journal of Australian Multicultural Society, 12*(1), 45–62.
Durán, R. J., & Campos, J. A. (2019). Gangs, gangsters, and the impact of settler colonialism on the Latina/o experience. *Sociology Compass, 14*(3). https://doi.org/10.1111/soc4.12765
Ekwe-Ekwe, H. (2006). *Biafra revisited*. African Renaissance.
Ewick, P., & Silbey, S. (1998). *The common place of law: Stories from everyday life*. University of Chicago Press.
Ewick, P., & Silbey, S. (2009). Narratives of law and legal consciousness. *Law & Society Review, 43*(4), 335–368.
Fadlalla Ali, A. H. (2009). *Customary law and legal pluralism in Sudan: An examination of the challenges of legal fragmentation*. Cambridge University Press.
Falola, T. (2020). *Decolonizing African knowledge: Autoethnography and African epistemologies*. Cambridge University Press.
Fanon, F. (1963). *The wretched of the earth*. Grove Press.
Farquharson, K., & Nolan, D. (2018). In a context of crime: Sudanese and South Sudanese Australians in the media. In D. Nolan, K. Farquharson, & T. Marjoribanks (Eds.), *Australian media and the politics of belonging* (pp. 85–104). Anthem Press.

Foley, R. (2011). Performing health in place: The Holy well as a therapeutic assemblage. *Health and Place, 17*(2), 470–479.

Forson, M. (2019). *The experiences of African Victorian young people. Findings and Recommendations report*. African Australian Community Taskforce.

Henriques-Gomes M. (2018, July 25). *'It's not safe for us': South Sudanese-Australians weather 'African gangs' storm.* https://www.theguardian.com/australia-news/2018/jul/25/its-not-safe-for-us-south-sudanese-australians-weather-african-gangs-storm

Higgins, R. (2011). The impact of colonial rule on African legal traditions: A historical analysis. *African Studies Review, 54*(2), 67–89.

Horák, M., Lacko, D., & Klocek, A. (2021). *Legal consciousness and everyday law: A socio-legal perspective.* Routledge.

Hunter, R. (2018). Indigenous legal issues, policing, and incarceration in Australia. *Australian Journal of Social Issues, 53*(3), 314–331.

Jakubowicz, A. (2018). Race, multiculturalism and the refugee crisis in Australia. *Journal of Ethnic and Migration Studies, 44*(1), 65–82.

Johnson, D. H. (2011). Colonialism and its consequences: African governance in transition. *Journal of African History, 52*(3), 421–439.

Jok, J. M. (2011). *War and the state: The transformation of governance in Africa.* University of Indiana Press.

Majavu, M. (2020). The 'African gangs' narrative: Associating blackness with criminality and other anti-Black racist tropes in Australia. *African and Black Diaspora: An International Journal, 12*(1), 27–39.

Mamdani, M. (1996). *Citizen and subject: Contemporary Africa and the legacy of late colonialism.* Princeton University Press.

Mamdani, M. (2001). *When victims become killers: Colonialism, nativism, and the genocide in Rwanda.* Princeton University Press.

Markus, A. (2016). *Australians today.* https://scanloninstitute.org.au/publication/australians-today

Massoud, M. F. (2013). *Law's fragility: Customary justice and colonial rule in Sudan.* Cambridge University Press.

Mbembe, A. (2001). *On the postcolony.* University of California Press.

Mbembe, A. (2017). *Critique of black reason.* Duke University Press.

Molla, T. (2019). Educational aspirations and experiences of refugee-background African youth in Australia: a case study. *International Journal of Inclusive Education, 25*(8), 877–895. https://doi.org/10.1080/13603116.2019.1588924

Muchoki, S. M. (2013). "(In Australia) what comes first are the women, then children, cats, dogs, followed by men": Exploring accounts of gender relations by men from the Horn of Africa. *Australasian Review of African Studies, 34*(2), 78.

Mungai, N., & Pease, B. (2009). Rethinking masculinities in the African diaspora: A study of African migrant men in Australia. *Journal of Intercultural Studies, 30*(2), 173–186.

Nair, R., & Vollhardt, J. R. (2020). Intersectionality and relations between oppressed groups: Intergroup implications of beliefs about intersectional differences and commonalities. *Journal of Social Issues, 76*(4), 993–1013. https://doi.org/10.1111/josi.12409

Ndlovu-Gatsheni, S. J. (2013). *Coloniality of power in postcolonial Africa: Myths of decolonization.* CODESRIA.

Nielsen, B. G. (2005). Book Review: Victimisation—Theory, Research and Policy. *Acta Sociologica, 48*(1), 91–93. https://doi.org/10.1177/000169930504800108 (Original work published 2005)

Nielsen, L., & Nieson, P. (2005). Law in everyday life: Perceptions and realities. *Stanford Law Review, 57*(2), 789–812.

Nunn, C. (2010). Spaces of exile: The politics of belonging for Sudanese refugees in Australia. *Journal of Intercultural Studies, 31*(2), 183–198.

Nyamnjoh, F. B. (2017). *Incompleteness: An African perspective.* Langaa RPCIG.

Panahi, R. (2016, July 10). *Lawless thugs terrorizing Melbourne.* Herald Sun, p.1.

Paradies, Y. C. (2006). Beyond black and white, essentialism, hybridity and indigeneity. *Journal of Sociology, 42*(4), 355–367.

Pittaway, E., & Bartolomei, L. (2001). Refugees, race, and gender: The multiple discrimination against refugee women. *Refuge: Canada's Journal on Refugees, 19*(6), 21–32.

Pittaway, E., & Muli, C. (2009). *'We have a voice—hear us': The settlement experiences of refugees and migrants from the Horn of Africa.* Refugee Council of Australia.

Pittaway, E., Muli, C., & Shteir, S. (2022). The refugee experience: Continuities of violence and intersectionality in forced migration. *Journal of Refugee Studies, 35*(2), 1–19.

Poljski, C. (2011). *On her way: Primary prevention of violence against immigrant and refugee women in Australia.* Multicultural Centre for Women's Health.

Rodney, W. (1972). *How Europe underdeveloped Africa.* Bogle-L'Ouverture Publications.

Sachs, A. (2013). The judicial role of African chiefs under colonial rule. *Journal of Legal Pluralism, 45*(1), 75–99.

Sehmi, A. (2024). Legacies of colonial violence in contemporary transitional justice: Memories of Mau Mau, the 'Kapenguria Six' and the 'Ocampo Six' in Kenya. *International Journal of Transitional Justice, 18*(1), 32–48. https://doi.org/10.1093/ijtj/ijae005

Scheper-Hughes, N., & Bourgois, P. (2004). *Violence in war and peace: An anthology*. Blackwell Publishing.

Shepherd, S. M., & Spivak, B. L. (2020). Estimating the extent and nature of offending by Sudanese-born individuals in Victoria. *Australian and New Zealand Journal of Criminology, 53*(3), 352–368. https://doi.org/10.1177/0004865820929066

Silbey, S. (2005). After legal consciousness. *Annual Review of Law and Social Science, 1*(1), 323–368.

Tilbury, F. (2007). 'I feel I am a bird without wings': Discourses of sadness and loss among East African refugees in Western Australia. *Identities, 14*(4), 433–458.

Udah, H. (2019). 'I belong here': African Australians' sense of belonging in regional Australia. *Australian Journal of Social Issues, 54*(4), 435–457.

Udah, H. (2023). Anti-black racism and othering: An exploration of the lived experience of black Africans who live in Australia. *Social Identities, 29*(2), 185–204. https://doi.org/10.1080/13504630.2023.2208056

Watkins E., Sood K. (2017, April 21). Did the Herald sun invent the Sudanese youth Apex gang? *Crikey*. https://www.crikey.com.au/2017/04/21/did-the-herald-sun-invent-the-sudanese-youth-apex-gang/

Weber, L. (2018). *'Police are good for some people, but not for Us': Community perspectives on young people, policing and belonging in greater Dandenong and casey*. Monash University.

Westoby, P. (2008). Legal consciousness and migrant communities: Understanding law in cultural contexts. *Journal of Migration Studies, 14*(2), 215–230.

3

Drivers of Family Violence in the South Sudanese Community

Introduction

Chapter 1 introduces the book, while Chapter 2 provides context about African Australian communities. It explores their migration patterns, settlement experiences in Australia, and the challenges and experiences of violence. In this chapter, I will present findings regarding the factors contributing to family violence within the South Sudanese community in Australia.

One of the objectives of this research was to identify the key drivers of family violence in the South Sudanese community. The findings reveal that the factors influencing family violence are diverse and complex. However, in the in-depth interviews, the identified drivers were linked to cultural, social, and economic experiences, traumatic post-migration war experiences, and the negative impact of settlement on mental health. While some of these factors found in mainstream and other refugee communities in studies such as (Boxall et al., 2022; Robinson et al., 2020; Spangaro et al., 2024; Webster et al., 2018), South Sudanese family dynamics and relationships are more intricate than simple cause-and-effect explanations. Although the driving factors behind family

A. K. Anyieth, *Decolonising Family Violence Legal Intervention Orders in African-Australian Communities*, https://doi.org/10.1007/978-3-031-95404-7_3

violence bear similarities to those found in many communities, they are also shaped by factors unique to the South Sudanese community.

Therefore, when I refer to 'drivers' in this context, I aim to encompass structural inequalities, racism, community attitudes, social and cultural norms, as well as beliefs and histories of violence, including pre-migration factors. These elements can be explained through psychology, which, broadly speaking, seeks to understand the psychological forces underlying participants' behaviours (Yakeley, 2018). For instance, historical violence, trauma, mental health challenges, and pre—and post-migration experiences in Australia manifest in harmful and destructive behaviours (Catani, 2010). There is also a clear relationship between these social experiences and individual behaviours.

This chapter presents an original analysis of the factors influencing family violence in the South Sudanese community, drawing upon themes emerging from interviews. The findings are based on accounts from South Sudanese individuals who have experienced family violence—either as recipients of Family Violence Intervention Orders or as family members affected by such violence. As such, this chapter provides unique insights into the factors contributing to violence that has been recognised by the Australian legal system as "family violence" warranting intervention, though not necessarily an immediate criminal justice response. The factors identified by South Sudanese participants include the effects of acculturation, changing gender roles, socioeconomic stressors (such as financial hardship), trauma (both individual and collective), and other pre-arrival experiences.

Effect of Acculturation

> *Adau, female participant:* In this context, communities vary significantly, cultures diverge, and everything is distinctly different. Our cultural landscape is undergoing transformation. Within our community, some individuals have rapidly assimilated into the ways of this country, while others strive to preserve our heritage. This contrast is often evident even within a single family.

In this research, the influence of cultural differences on family violence and its intersection with Australian law is a recurring theme across the research data. Therefore, culture and cultural practices are recurring threads throughout this and the following discussion chapters. In this chapter, the process of South Sudanese acculturation is discussed as one of the driving factors of family violence.

Culture is a learned behaviour shared and passed from one generation to the next for human adjustment and adaptation (Milner & Khawaja, 2010). It encompasses institutions, social norms, roles, values, and beliefs through learned behaviours (Tempany, 2009), forming an integral part of an individual's life and shaping their understanding of the world. Over the years, efforts have been made to assimilate various cultural groups into the dominant white settler society, rooted in British colonial culture (Dandy & Pe-Pua, 2013). Australian culture predominantly remains individualistic, where the person is viewed as independent of others within the framework of the dominant white Australian culture (Dandy & Pe-Pua, 2013).

South Sudanese refugees, having grown up in one cultural context, are required to rebuild their lives in a new cultural environment upon migration (Milner & Khawaja, 2010). Consequently, their journey involves a complex interplay of continuity and change, including a process of acculturation (Berry, 1997). Acculturation, as defined by Redfield et al. (1936, p. 149), refers to the phenomena that arise when groups of individuals from different cultures come into continuous firsthand contact, resulting in changes in the original cultural patterns of either or both groups (as cited in Berry, 1997, p. 7). This process affects not only how the migrating community interacts with the host society but also how they relate within their own communities and personal lives (Milner & Khawaja, 2010).

Participants in this research discussed cultural shifts and evolving gender roles as factors contributing to family violence within the South Sudanese community. Some attributed this to women's empowerment and gender equality, which they perceived as giving women more power than men in Australian society (Abur & Mphande, 2019). However, acculturation should not be viewed solely in terms of changing cultural practices and gender roles. It is a broader process with various adaptation outcomes that impact South Sudanese families (Khawaja & Milner, 2012), which can be categorised as psychological adaptation, psychological well-being, socio-cultural adaptation, and socioeconomic adaptation.

Psychological adaptation and well-being refer to health and life satisfaction within the acculturating group, while socio-cultural adaptation involves acquiring the necessary social skills to integrate into the new cultural setting and engage successfully in social interactions (Ward, 2001). Socio-psychological adaptation relates to shifts in values, identities, and intergroup attitudes, shaping how individuals perceive themselves and others (Mähönen & Jasinskaja-Lahti, 2013). Economic adaptation, on the other hand, pertains to how migrants obtain employment and whether their work is fulfilling and effective within the new culture (Berry, 1997). For example, a South Sudanese migrant who previously held a high-status, well-paying professional career in their home country but is now limited to low-paid, low-status jobs such as factory work in Australia may experience a loss of status and earning capacity. This, in turn, can negatively affect their mental health and sense of self-worth in society (Abdelkerim & Grace, 2012; Abur, 2016).

The impact of acculturation on South Sudanese gender norms is a significant concern raised by participants in this research. Both respondents and applicants argued that cultural changes should not be seen as an inherent cause of family violence but rather as part of a broader context involving numerous adaptations and adjustments. These include compromises, sacrifices, shifts in roles, careers, and social experiences that reshape identities. It is these changes, coupled with South Sudanese cultural beliefs, that drive experiences of family violence.

> *Mary, female participant:* I was working long hours and coming home very late, which he did not appreciate. If I didn't work, his income wouldn't be enough to support us here and our family overseas. He often insisted that a "South Sudanese woman shouldn't stay out until ungodly hours—it's not in our culture". We argued about that frequently.

Participants noted that in South Sudanese culture, specific expectations and behavioural rules for men and women differ from Western norms (Khawaja & Milner, 2012). Traditionally, South Sudanese men are expected to be the heads of the family, holding dominant roles within the household, while women are expected to take on caregiving responsibilities and oversee family well-being (Deng, 2016). While these gender roles may be seen as patriarchal from a Western perspective, they provide structure in terms of family operations and fulfilment of expected duties (Khawaja & Milner, 2012).

However, these gender dynamics are challenged upon resettlement in Australia, where significant efforts are made to promote gender equality and challenge traditional practices perceived as subordinating women. This cultural conflict was highlighted in interviews, with one participant, Garang, expressing:

> *Garang, male participant:* You understand that what we are doing is not the same as what white people here do. It is because of their culture; it is within their rights. They do not behave as we do now. Yes, some of them engage in this [family violence], but others do not. For us, as I mentioned, we experience a 'cultural shock,' which is why people are acting out of order and against our culture. Overcoming this cultural shock is very challenging. Women are learning this new culture, involving the police, and even forcing men out of their homes. Now, our women are in control, while the men find themselves in a vulnerable position. So, where is the balance here? This is not how it was back home. We will do our best to bring our people together, educate them about what is happening, and work towards preventing this [family violence] from occurring.

Garang's observations highlight how South Sudanese men and women are affected differently by cultural change and the challenges that come with it, despite experiencing the same transition. While shifting gender roles are acknowledged as part of acculturation, particularly in how men and women navigate this process, they will be explored further below as a driving factor.

Although Garang recognises the role of South Sudanese patriarchal culture in experiences of family violence, some participants described cultural practices and traditions as the only symbols of continuity in an otherwise constantly changing world shaped by displacement and migration due to the civil war.

> *Achol, female participant:* Our culture has always endured, but it is different here. Things are changing rapidly, and this is affecting many couples. I am not certain of the exact reason, but our community is deteriorating every day. Nowadays, separations and divorces are becoming increasingly common.

These cultural practices are now colliding with and being challenged by mainstream Australian culture, laws, and systems. However, before migration, these practices were effective in providing families with a functional structure and preserving family units, leading to fewer breakdowns and divorces among pre-migration South Sudanese families (Deng, 2016). When the continuity of cultural norms is disrupted, friction arises within families. The experience of having South Sudanese traditions challenged by a new culture may be having negative consequences within the former refugee and migrant community.

> *Akuol, female participant:* I am young and want to live my life, but he was controlling about everywhere I went. He wanted me to stay in the house and "be a good South Sudanese woman," but I wanted to go out sometimes.

These findings align with studies conducted by Khawaja and Melner (2012) and Abur (2019; 2023), which examined South Sudanese settlement challenges and acculturation stressors in Australia. Both studies found that acculturation stress can influence marital relationships in the context of individual adaptation to cultural change. Family dynamics and the strategies each partner employs can contribute to conflict. Conflict may also arise when one partner, holding onto South Sudanese traditions and cultural practices regarding family, struggles to adapt to mainstream Australian culture. This conflict becomes more pronounced when the other partner, having already adapted to the dominant host culture, is expected to adhere to pre-migration values and traditions (Milner & Khawaja, 2010).

As a result, a less acculturated husband or wife may perceive the behaviour of the more highly acculturated partner as a threat, increasing their level of acculturative stress and leading to conflict (Lee & Liu, 2001). These cultural shifts have contributed to an increase in family breakdown and divorce within the South Sudanese community, as explained by participants such as Thon and Alek, who stated that:

> *Thon, male participant:* When we were back home [South Sudan] and in Egypt, things were not like they are now. There has been a lot of change in our community, and I can't say all of it is good.
> *Alek, female participant:* When we left our land, everything had already fallen apart, and people were fighting, but we were not like we are now. We hoped to find some rest and peace in the West, but finding rest here has become even harder for us. Now, 24 hours a day, children are on the streets, parents are fighting, divorces happen quickly and easily, some end up in prison, and children—who should not even know about death—are witnessing their peers dying. Clearly, South Sudanese culture and Australian culture have clashed. You know, the cultures have clashed.

Thon and Alek's quotes highlight the multiple ways in which the new cultural experience affects families, from parents to children and young people. This suggests that settlement acculturation places stress on marital and family relationships when individuals within families adapt to life in Australia at different rates. Many individuals experience changes in gendered family dynamics as part of settlement acculturation, which can be perceived as a loss of cultural identity (Khawaja & Milner, 2012). Acculturation progresses at different speeds within individual families, affecting both young people and parents (Pittaway et al., 2022). These shifts generate tension and may contribute to conditions conducive to family violence (Pittaway et al., 2022).

Additionally, these shifts may disrupt pre-existing roles based on South Sudanese cultural beliefs, expectations, and practices within families and between men and women, particularly in intimate relationships.

In summary, participants' observations align with research findings that acculturation—through adjustments to culture, as well as changes in gender roles, social status, and employment—places pressure on relationships. Their insights provide a nuanced understanding of how acculturation can be a driver of family violence within the South Sudanese community.

Changing Gender Roles

Changing gender roles play a significant role in contributing to experiences of family violence within the South Sudanese community. As traditional gender norms shift, particularly with migration and settlement in Australia, tensions arise between old cultural expectations and new social realities. Men may feel threatened by changes in power dynamics, especially as women gain more independence and autonomy. This shift can result in frustration and insecurity, sometimes manifesting as violence. For women, adjusting to evolving gender roles can also lead to confusion and conflict as they navigate expectations both within their community and in broader Australian society. These changing dynamics contribute to the complex nature of family violence in South Sudanese households.

> *Nyamar, female participant:* I asked him to help me make dinner because I was tied. He almost fainted at the thought of me suggesting that he cook. In South Sudanese culture, it's uncommon for a woman to send her husband into the kitchen; the roles are very clearly defined. Here, things are more flexible, and the traditional expectations are less strict, but our men, especially the older ones, don't want this change to happen.

Participants confirmed some assumptions about African patriarchies but demonstrated a more nuanced awareness of the specific patterns, practices, and manifestations of gender roles. Both male and female participants identified that gender roles in many South Sudanese households were rigidly defined before migration. Traditionally, men were expected to be the breadwinners and decision-makers, while women were responsible for homemaking and child-rearing (Marlowe et al., 2014; Carlton & Russell, 2015). The responsibility for protecting and providing for the family rested upon the man, not the woman (Marlowe et al., 2014). As Deng (2016) explains, men held the most authority within the family, community, and society.

As discussed by Duany and Duany (2001) in War and Women in Sudan, these structures and the role of men were not intended to subordinate women but to honour and protect them from performing heavy duties beyond nurturing and caring for the children and family. Traditionally, South Sudanese women assumed multiple roles within the family, including wife, leader, administrator, and manager of family wealth. As mothers, they were seen as the central figures holding the family unit together (Duany & Duany, 2001). Their caregiving and nurturing duties were highly regarded—not as signs of weakness, but as honourable positions contributing to a higher quality of family life (Duany & Duany, 2001). However, these roles are now shifting in Australia, disrupting pre-existing family structures and causing friction between intimate partners and family members as both men and women struggle to adjust to Western constructs of gender roles (Khawaja & Milner, 2012).

Although efforts to equalise gender roles are important, they can become problematic when influenced by colonial ideologies surrounding family, gender equality, and the roles of men and women (Sylvester, 1995). This perspective often portrays women as powerless and assumes that most men hold power and subordinate women, thereby undermining certain cultural practices that empower women by granting them self-determination and agency in non-Western cultures (Byrne, 2020). Furthermore, this standpoint pays little attention to the racism and discrimination that both African men and women face in areas such as education and employment in Australia, as well as to systemic barriers that undermine the role of African men (Anyieth, 2021).

A key shift in gender roles is the growing expectation for South Sudanese women to work in Australia due to economic pressures, social isolation, and a lack of support. In many African cultures, particularly in South Sudan, women working outside the home were not widely supported. This shift makes some men feel as though they are losing their traditional role within the family (Boonzaier & de la Rey, 2004). Many experience a sense of shame when they believe they are failing to fulfil their social obligations as breadwinners and heads of the family, particularly if they are forced to rely on financial welfare assistance (Deng, 2016).

Participants recognised that the traditional paternalistic attitudes surrounding gender roles in South Sudanese families have carried over into their lives in Australia. Both male and female participants expressed their perspectives on this transition. Below, I include three quotes—one from a female participant and two from male participants—to capture both genders' experiences, expectations, and understandings of gender roles within South Sudanese families.

> *Achol, female participant:* Most responsibilities outside the home belonged to men. They were the ones who farmed the land, harvested crops, and stored them. Then it was the women's turn to fetch or collect from the storage. Everything within the house was under the woman's control. She knew what was available, what was lacking, and the challenges the family faced. That was how it was in the past.
>
> *John, male participant:* I was the breadwinner back home. I provided for my family, including my extended family. I protected my family during the difficult journey through many countries until we arrived here, but now it's very different. Now, I feel like I am the woman, and my wife is the man.
>
> *Thon, male participant:* I never wanted my wife to work outside the home because it goes against our culture, and it makes me feel like a weak man who cannot provide for my family. My income is not sufficient, and I don't want to rely on Centrelink to support us. In many families in our community, Centrelink effectively becomes the husband, leading to a lack of respect for men. Some women even say, "You can leave; Centrelink will take care of me and the kids." I didn't want to hear that from my wife.

Both Achol, John, and Thon confirmed the cultural and traditional expectations of gender roles within South Sudanese families. These reflections support previous research into the attitudes of men from Horn of Africa refugee communities (including Sudan, Somalia, Ethiopia, and Eritrea), which found that they experienced shifts in gender roles and dynamics that differed considerably from those in their countries of origin, affecting their intimate lives and family relationships (Muchoki, 2013; Ndhlovu, 2014).

Women and children are considered to be at high risk of family violence when the male partner or father, who strongly identifies with traditional patriarchal norms and rigid masculine identities, begins to perceive them as disempowering agents or as participants in changing family roles. This challenge to patriarchal and rigid gender dynamics increases the risk of family violence. The perception of women as changing—or at least transforming—as they pursue formal education and economic independence in Western countries has challenged many rigidly defined South Sudanese cultural norms and inadvertently affected South Sudanese family units.

Moreover, most participants, both male and female, observed that more South Sudanese women are reconsidering traditional gender roles upon moving to Australia. Living in a more feminist-driven society, where Western ideas about gender equality are prevalent, has created tensions between individual rights in the West and the African traditions of collectivism that have been shared and passed down through generations, as highlighted by Alek and Mayen.

> *Alek, female participant:* There are many changes in our community—women are changing, men are changing, and young people are changing. But sometimes, too much change is not good, as we can see in our community and how things are now. Most men do not like this change.
> *Mayen, male participant:* Of course, men are struggling in this country. The law here has placed men at the bottom of the family hierarchy. They are no longer the head; everything revolves around what the woman says. In this country, African men are at the bottom of almost everything. They are at the bottom at home and at the bottom in the job market.

Participants view this as a driver of family violence and as a means for men to regain a sense of authority within the family. This aligns with El-Murr's (2018) research on intimate partner violence in Australian refugee communities and, more specifically, with Deng's (2016) findings on family dynamics and gender roles, particularly the role of men in families. In this research, men who understood their role as the sole providers, protectors, and heads of the household—such as Atem—expressed that the increasing social power of women, combined with Australian family law as a system for resolving family conflicts, makes men who strongly identify with rigid masculine norms feel as though they have lost their masculine identities.

> *Atem, male participant:* Back home, men worked and provided for the family; they protected the family and handled everything outside the home. Now, in Australia, these roles are mixed, and men are losing their wives and children in the process. Wives no longer respect them, and children no longer listen to their elders. As a man, sitting at home or providing so little for your family is frustrating.

As Atem highlighted, men who strongly identify with traditional masculine identities—shaped by cultural norms that define rigid gender roles—understood their role as the sole providers for the family. However, existing literature in Australia demonstrates that Black men, such as South Sudanese Australian men, face numerous barriers in the job market and education. Racism prevents them from gaining other forms of social status and power (Abur, 2016).

Thus, the perpetration of family violence can be seen as a way for some men to reclaim their sense of manhood. It becomes an accessible option when other avenues are closed. Extensive literature (Anderson & Umberson, 2001; Our Watch, 2019; Mshweshwe, 2020; Flood et al., 2022) supports the argument that family violence is an expression of male dominance and toxic masculinity. This is often manifested through controlling and abusing those closest to them, particularly intimate partners and other family members (Khawaja & Milner, 2012).

However, viewing masculinity as the sole explanation for family violence is overly simplistic. Researchers must consider the social and structural inequalities experienced by African men and families. As mentioned earlier, traditional South Sudanese gender roles dictate that men are the breadwinners and decision-makers, while women are home-makers and child-bearers. However, being able to provide requires employment or other means of securing resources for one's family. The lack of such opportunities for many South Sudanese families is a significant concern among this research's participants. The inability to provide has not only placed families in hardship but has also contributed to family violence within the South Sudanese community, as participants explain in the following section.

Resources and Financial Hardship

There is no doubt that family violence is deeply rooted in power imbalances between men and women, as well as in social and gender inequalities (Victorian Government, 2021). However, these imbalances are reinforced by the unequal distribution of resources in Australia. The lack of resources has long been recognised as a driving factor in family violence and is more prevalent in some communities than in others (Antai et al., 2014).

Similar to Abur and Spaaij's (2016) study, Mungai and Gitau (2019) examined the challenges faced by African Australian individuals regarding unemployment and the benefits of employment. This research's findings confirm that discrimination in employment, educational institutions, and other sectors that shape human life experiences has increased inequality for many African families compared to other migrant communities and white families. Participants such as Nyamar, Mayen, and John-S recognised that family violence is partly linked to economic inequalities between migrant families, such as the South Sudanese, and more economically established cohorts in Australia. Moreover, it is associated with practices of hegemonic or toxic masculinity.

> *Nyamar, female participant:* I say yes, our men can be quite violent, but you can't compare their lives and access to life-fulfilling resources with other non-former refugee men. These men came from nothing to nothing—some from broken homes, with missing and angry fathers. My husband was violent; he took all his pain out on us, and I was afraid my sons would copy that one day. But I also worry for him because, even now, his life is worse—he doesn't have a job.
>
> *Mayen, male participant:* I struggled to find a stable job for months. Living off Centrelink (social welfare) is not enough, and it's shameful for a strong and capable man like myself to be dependent on Centrelink.

> The money is never enough for one family here, let alone for those who have extended families to support back home.
> *John-S, male participant:* Things were tough, especially when children came along. Nothing was ever enough for my wife and children; it broke me, and it caused a lot of fights between me and my wife. I gave up. I don't bother looking for an office job anymore. I am trying to be content with factory work because that is where I can at least make the small amount of money I earn.

There is consensus among Nyamar, Mayen, and John-S that financial hardship and a lack of self-fulfilment ultimately contribute to family violence. Recognising these intersecting cultural, economic, social, and psychological dynamics reveals that family violence within South Sudanese families cannot be attributed solely to gender imbalance or patriarchy but must also be understood in the context of their economic deprivation as migrants in a colonial and capitalist society.

In this context, a lack of sustainable employment has led to financial hardship within families. As Colic-Peisker and Tilbury (2007) and Abur (2017) found, despite a large proportion of African Australians—especially those who recently migrated from refugee backgrounds—having professional qualifications, many face employment barriers due in part to racism and discrimination in Australian job markets. My participants' accounts of financial hardships align with findings from other recent studies, such as Dut (2021), who explored the experiences of African Australian migrant families during the COVID-19 pandemic in Melbourne.

> *Deng, male participant:* Our community has faced significant challenges, which worsened during the pandemic. Many people lost their jobs, particularly those in manufacturing and warehousing. You know, when you're employed as a casual or part-time worker, you are always the first to be laid off.

In addition to financial hardship, many African families in Australia bear the added burden of transnational care through 'Black Tax'. This refers to the financial responsibility of supporting family members both in Australia and in their home countries, creating a distinctive financial strain compared to families whose obligations are confined to their nuclear households within Australia. These additional responsibilities place Australian-based families at greater financial risk, increasing stress levels and fostering feelings of hopelessness. Many recently arrived African Australian families, such as the South Sudanese, have deeply communal traditions, which translate into providing for extended family members. However, due to limited opportunities, particularly for men, many South Sudanese individuals no longer find their purpose solely in being the primary breadwinner, protector, or provider for their families.

Atem and Lisa elaborated on this concept. Once again, I include extended extracts to fully represent the experiences of my participants. The inclusion of longer excerpts provides context, amplifies participants' voices, and enriches their narratives. Atem's description of financial pressures illustrates the direct connections, as perceived by participants, between limited resources, family violence, and the consequences they face as a result.

> *Atem, male participant:* The first thing that happened when I lost my job was the loss of my value and respect in the eyes of my ex-wife, extended family, and community. They would no longer listen to me, even if I had a valid point; it was as if I had become an outcast and a vagabond. I was seen as a drunkard and an irresponsible person. At one point, the doctor advised me to move out of Melbourne due to my inability to find work and the cold weather, which affected my health, so I moved to Perth. When I returned to pick up my wife and children, she refused. I suggested that we take the kids to my mum's place while we both found jobs, or that we rent a house and bring my mum in to take care of the children while we worked. She refused because she did not like my mother. It was frustrating to be a man and to be unable to fulfil my economic duties because providing for your family defines you as a provider. At this point, I became so frustrated that I turned to drinking like never before. One day, I came home late, and she stopped me at the door, refusing to let me in. Out of anger and frustration, I slapped her, and she took me to court [meaning they received a Family Violence Intervention Order (FVIO)]. This incident has had a profound impact on my life. I am sorry to say

this, but even sexually, I am not as active anymore. In simple terms, I am traumatised.

Atem's account demonstrates how job loss and financial pressures can trigger persistent mental and physical health issues, contributing to violence and long-term health conditions. Following his job loss, his family disintegrated, and he experienced a loss of standing within the community. This, in turn, led to excessive alcohol consumption, resulting in adverse mental and physical health outcomes. Lisa's perspective reinforces the financial strains that Atem discussed but from a woman's point of view.

Lisa, female participant: You see, the man has had children with you, yet he is unable to raise or support them financially because he keeps saying, 'I don't have a job.' If the government would listen to the people, I believe it could help these men secure stable jobs and set them up for child support so they can contribute financially to raising their children.

Lisa highlights some of the key challenges related to financial instability within families, particularly among separated or divorced partners. While these factors may not directly cause family violence, they add an extra layer of stress exacerbated by financial difficulties. Firstly, Lisa concurs with Atem regarding the economic struggles faced by some African men in Australia. Secondly, men find themselves unable to provide for their children due to unfavourable financial circumstances resulting from unemployment. However, within the context of rigid cultural beliefs and patriarchal practices, many South Sudanese women may remain in violent relationships partly due to the stigma associated with being labelled a single mother. These combined experiences are interconnected and contribute to family violence within the South Sudanese community.

While wives and children may feel that their husbands and fathers are depriving them of essential provisions and protection, many South Sudanese men are grappling with financial crises not only for themselves but also for their extended families and the broader community.

This lack of adequate economic support results in an absence of fulfilment and a crisis of purpose, as Atem recounted earlier. Consequently, this contributes to experiences of family violence and poor mental health conditions. These findings underscore the interplay between social inequalities, limited socioeconomic opportunities, and the perpetration of family violence, supporting the discussion on the intersections of violence within African Australian communities in Chapter 2.

This research suggests that social structures, lack of employment, and the erosion of cultural identity combine to create a sense of inferiority among many South Sudanese families. These experiences are closely tied to feelings of powerlessness, loss of social identity, frustration, anger, and a diminished sense of self-worth. Ultimately, these factors significantly contribute to poor mental health conditions, family breakdowns, and both the victimisation and perpetration of family violence.

Pre-migration Trauma

The cultural background of many South Sudanese individuals and families in Australia is rooted in colonial violence, war, conflict, displacement, migration, and the search for better opportunities for self-actualisation (Copping & Shakespeare-Finch, 2013; Khawaja et al., 2008; Schweitzer et al., 2006). These pre-migration hardships, further exacerbated by negative settlement experiences, have left many South Sudanese Australians grappling with Post-Traumatic Stress Disorder (PTSD) and overall poor mental health.

Pre-migration traumas are worsened by encounters with Family Violence Intervention Orders (FVIOs) and complex legal processes, as described by Mabior, Ajokdit, Atem, and Mary:

> *Mabior, male participant:* Many of us are now walking around mentally disoriented. They have become a mess; I have become a mess. Men whose wives have chased them away and gone with other men are seen as weak. They cannot stand on their own, and the shock can be so intense that it might disable them mentally rendering them unable to work. You find them just wandering aimlessly. Since we have been here, I don't think we

have found true peace and rest as some of us thought we would. Instead, when we encounter hardship in a place that was made to sound like a safe haven, we become sad and disappointed.
Ajokdit, male participant: You can see that many people are not mentally well, especially the men. I don't think doctors here truly grasp the extent of the mental health challenges in our community.
Atem, male participant: Something happened to me back home right before coming to Australia, and it affected my memory. I still forget things at times, which is stressful. I am still recovering to this day, and this issue has caused me a lot of stress, increased my blood pressure, and led to stomach problems.

Similar to the accounts of Mabior, Ajokdit, and Atem, Mary also highlights the mental health challenges faced by the South Sudanese Australian community:

Mary, female participant: Our people are experiencing a great deal of pain, which is evident in their behaviour. However, due to other greater and more pressing challenges, seeking mental health support has become a lesser priority for many. Additionally, sitting down one-on-one with someone to discuss personal problems is unfamiliar to many of us, leading to reluctance in pursuing therapy. This is particularly worse among South Sudanese men—they believe that to be a man is to never ask for help. This mindset is very damaging and is destroying many families.

Understanding the intricate psychological forces underlying certain behaviours within the South Sudanese community is of paramount importance in comprehending family violence and exploring potential interventions. The link between trauma and the perpetration of family violence has been well-documented in other communities that have experienced trauma and oppression. For instance, Herman (2022), who examines victims and survivors of family violence, and Atkinson (2002, 2008), who explores complex trauma among Indigenous populations subjected to historical violence, both make critical connections between experiences of violence and trauma.

Herman (2022) argues that experiencing complex trauma in some cases (though not all) increases the risk of struggling to manage stressful situations, sometimes leading to self-destructive or violent behaviour. The trauma lens provides a critical analysis of family violence, particularly in communities with histories of mass violence, highlighting contributing factors that may not be immediately visible.

Pre-arrival traumatic experiences significantly impact the ability of individuals from refugee backgrounds to adapt to a new environment, exacerbating family functioning issues both during and after settlement (El-Murr, 2018). Participants have emphasised the significance of psychological factors, particularly trauma, as a driving force behind family violence. The prevalence of PTSD within the South Sudanese community, especially among men, has been highlighted by Anyieth and Abur (2022) as a significant contributor to self-destructive behaviour and incidents of family violence. The intersection of pre-existing trauma with the social and economic pressures of life in Australia can trigger violent reactions due to overwhelming emotions stemming from these negative experiences, as described by Sarah and Tina:

> *Sarah, female participant:* We have been through a lot, and now people are extremely hot-tempered. They resort to beating each other up instead of talking—not because we were born like that, but partly due to everything we have experienced both pre—and post-migration.
> *Tina, female participant:* He managed the household as if he were still in the midst of war. His mindset resembled that of a commanding soldier—whatever he said had to be done. That's where our problems started. I confronted him, reminding him that he was no longer in the army and should stop exerting control and issuing orders in our home. Such controlling actions or behaviours are considered unacceptable in Australia and often lead to conflicts.

Tina and Sarah's accounts illustrate the challenges faced by many South Sudanese individuals living in Australia, where past experiences of violence and trauma intersect with limited social, economic, and psychological support. Many participants in this research link their changing environment and hardships to their hostility, whether as perpetrators or victims of various forms of violence.

From a Western psychological perspective, Sarah's narrative aligns with Post-Traumatic Stress Disorder (PTSD). According to Jones et al. (2001),

PTSD is a disorder that can be understood as a normal response to abnormal events. The diagnostic criteria for PTSD were introduced in the third edition of the DSM (DSM-III; American Psychiatric Association), formulated based on observations and interviews with male Vietnam War veterans (van der Kolk et al., 2005; Courtois, 2008). PTSD provided a framework for understanding how mental health is influenced by life events, acknowledging that symptoms arise in response to real experiences that overwhelm an individual's coping abilities.

Although Tina did not explicitly link her ex-husband's controlling behaviour to war veteran trauma, her statement—"he ran the house like he was still in the war"—strongly suggests that he was struggling with the transition to civilian life. This reaction is common among ex-combatants who have served in the military for extended periods. The participants' testimonies emphasise the significance of PTSD in discussions and efforts to prevent family violence.

Migrant families who have endured past conflicts, experienced the loss and injury of family members, lived in constant fear, faced immigration challenges, and struggled to adapt to a new society, social deprivation, and the uncertainty of refugee status, are at high risk of family breakdowns. Numerous studies, including Ramsay et al. (1993), Klarić et al. (2008), Marvasti (2012), Castro-Vale et al. (2019), Olff et al. (2025), and Ogunsiji et al. (2025) have established that trauma survivors experience varying degrees of acute and chronic trauma effects. These can manifest in multiple ways among war veterans and their families, including diminished psychological and psychosocial functioning, heightened psychological and physical pain symptoms, and disruptions in self-worth and social connections, as described by Garang:

> *Garang, male participant:* When we arrived, I was initially fine, but then I started having trouble sleeping, even when I was exhausted from work. This continued for a long time. I even had an accident on the road because my mind was elsewhere. So, I went to see the family doctor. He diagnosed it as something related to my mental health, although I can't recall the exact term. He prescribed medication to help me sleep and reduce my anxiety.

The intricate patterns of trauma exposure and their effects present challenges in making generalisations about the drivers of family violence. Therefore, it is crucial to challenge the dominant argument that men perpetrate family violence solely due to male privilege, power, and control. While these factors contribute to violent behaviour, they are not the sole or primary causes within the South Sudanese community. Instead, they intersect with numerous other drivers of violence, as explored earlier.

Understanding the co-occurring traumatic experiences and the broader context of migration is essential in shaping interventions and prevention strategies. Recognising the role of unemployment, discrimination, racism, and language barriers (Fauk et al., 2021) further highlights the complexities surrounding help-seeking and family violence experiences.

Conclusion

In conclusion, this chapter has provided a well-rounded understanding of the South Sudanese community's unique experiences and contributors to family violence. It begins by detailing the manifestations of family violence within South Sudanese families, particularly focusing on the forms of violence experienced and approaches to help-seeking. Participants' narratives suggest that families face numerous challenges both before and after settling in Australia, which contribute to family violence, gender inequalities, and patriarchal dynamics within family structures.

It was deduced that the process of acculturation impacts traditional practices and gender roles within families. This, in turn, introduces an element of separation and adaptation to Western norms and beliefs surrounding gender roles and family dynamics. Consequently, while many South Sudanese families grapple with redefining family structures, gender roles, and cultural norms, men often express feelings of disempowerment, leading to conflicts that culminate in family violence.

In addition to acculturation and gender roles, participants identified a lack of resources, particularly financial support within families, as a key contributor to family violence. This confluence of complex challenges results in diverse negative outcomes within families, making interventions and prevention strategies more complicated in the Australian context. Furthermore, the chapter concludes with a discussion on the role of pre—and post-migration trauma as contributing factors to experiences of violence within the South Sudanese community.

Having explored the contributing factors to family violence in the South Sudanese Australian community, the following chapter will examine traditional approaches to family violence intervention and prevention from an African customary law perspective.

References

Abdelkerim A. A., Grace M. (2012). Challenges to employment in newly emerging African communities in Australia: A review of the literature. *Australian Social Work, 65*(1), 104–119. https://doi.org/10.1080/0312407X.2011.616958

Abur, W. (2016). *Settlement strategies for the South Sudanese community in Australia: Social capital and the social fabric*. Scholars' Press.

Abur, W. (2019). *A new life with opportunities and challenges: the settlement experiences of South Sudanese Australians*. Deakin University. Book. https://hdl.handle.net/10536/DRO/DU:30133686

Abur, W. (2023). *Our voices understanding critical challenges of settlement when resettled in country different to your own country*. Deakin University. Book. https://hdl.handle.net/10536/DRO/DU:30132983

Abur, W., & Spaaij, R. (2016). Settlement and employment experiences of South Sudanese people from refugee backgrounds in Melbourne, Australia. *Australasian Review of African Studies, 37*(2), 107–128. https://doi.org/10.22160/22035184/aras-2016-37-2/107-128

Anderson, K. L., & Umberson, D. (2001). GENDERING VIOLENCE: Masculinity and Power in Men's Accounts of Domestic Violence. *Gender & Society, 15*(3), 358–380. https://doi.org/10.1177/089124301015003003 (Original work published 2001).

Antai, D., Antai, J., & Anthony, D. S. (2014). The relationship between socio-economic inequalities, intimate partner violence and economic abuse: A national study of women in the Philippines. *Global Public Health, 9*, 808–826. *Applied Psychology, 46*(1), 5–34.

Anyieth, A. K. (2021). *South sudanese manhood and family crisis in the diaspora.* Africa World Book.

Anyieth, A. K., & Abur, W. (2022). The war trauma and mental health challenges for South Sudanese men in the Diaspora. *People centred—The Journal of Development Administration (JDA), 7*(3), 75–83.

Atkinson, J. (2002). *Trauma trails: Recreating song lines: The transgenerational effects of trauma in Indigenous Australia.* Spinifex Press.

Berry, J. W. (1997). Immigration, acculturation, and adaptation. *Applied Psychology: An International Review, 46*(1), 5–34. https://doi.org/10.1080/026999497378467

Boonzaier, F., & de la Rey, C. (2004). Woman Abuse: The Construction of Gender in Women and Men's Narratives of Violence. *South African Journal of Psychology, 34*, 443–463.

Boxall, H., Doherty, L., Lawler, S., Franks, C., & Bricknell, S. (2022). *The "Pathways to intimate partner homicide" project: Key stages and events in male-perpetrated intimate partner homicide in Australia* (Research report, 04/2022). ANROWS.

Byrne, D. (2020). Decolonial African feminism for white allies. *Journal of International Women's Studies, 21*(7), 37–46. Available at: https://vc.bridgew.edu/jiws/vol21/iss7/4

Carlton, B., & Russell, E. (2015). *'A gender for change': Cycles of women's penal reform and reconfigurations of anti-prison resistance in Victoria, Australia.* Champ Pénal XII.

Castro-Vale, I., Severo, M., Carvalho, D., & Mota-Cardoso, R. (2019). Intergenerational transmission of war-related trauma assessed 40 years after exposure. *Annals of General Psychiatry, 18*(1). https://doi.org/10.1186/s12991-019-0238-2

Catani, C. (2010). War at Home—a Review of the Relationship between War Trauma and Family Violence. *VERHALTENSTHERAPIE, 20*(1), 1. https://doi.org/10.1159/000261994

Copping, A., Shakespeare-Finch, J. (2013). Trauma and survival in African humanitarian entrants to Australia. In K. Gow, M. Celinski (Eds.), *Natural disaster research, prediction and mitigation. Mass trauma: Impact and recovery issues* (pp. 331–347). Nova Science Publishers.

Colic-Peisker, V., & Tilbury, F. (2007). Integration into the Australian Labour Market: The Experience of Three 'Visibly Different' Groups of Recently Arrived Refugees. *International Migration, [online] 45*(1), 59–85. https://doi.org/10.1111/j.1468-2435.2007.00396.x

Courtois, C. A. (2008). Complex trauma, complex reactions: Assessment and treatment. *Psychological Trauma: Theory, Research, Practice, and Policy, S(1)*, 86–100. https://doi.org/10.1037/1942-9681.S.1.86

Dandy, J., & Pe-Pua, R. (2013). Beyond mutual acculturation: Intergroup relations among immigrants, Anglo-Australians, and indigenous Australians. *Zeitschrift für Psychologie, 221*(4), 232–241. https://doi.org/10.1027/2151-2604/a000153

Deng, S., A. (2016). *South Sudanese family dynamics and parenting practices in Australia.* Proceedings of the 38th AFSAAP Conference: 21st Century Tensions and Transformation Africa. Deakin University: African Studies Association of Australasia and the Pacific (AFSAAP).

Duany, J. A., & Duany, W. (2001). War and Women in the Sudan: Role change and adjustment to new responsibilities. *Northeast African Studies, 8*(2), 63–82. https://doi.org/10.1353/nas.2005.0024

Dut, G. M. (2021). The experience of South Sudanese migrant families during the COVID-19 pandemic in Melbourne. *Australian and New Zealand Journal of Public Health, 45*(5), 427–429. https://doi.org/10.1111/1753-6405.13134

El-Murr, A. (2018). Intimate Partner Violence in Australian Refugee Communities. https://aifs.gov.au/cfca/publications/cfca-paper/intimate-partner-violence-australian-refugee-communities

Flood, M., Brown, C., Dembele, L., & Mills, K. (2022). Who uses domestic, family, and sexual violence, how, and why? *The State of Knowledge Report on Violence Perpetration.* Brisbane: Queensland University of Technology.

Herman, J. L. (2022). *Trauma and Recovery: The Aftermath of Violence–from Domestic Abuse to Political Terror*. Paperback ed. New York: Basic Books.

Jones, C., Griffiths, R. D., Humphris, G., & Skirrow, P. M. (2001). Memory, delusions, and the development of acute posttraumatic stress disorder-related symptoms after intensive care. *Critical Care Medicine, 29*(3), 573–580. https://doi.org/10.1097/00003246-200103000-00019

Khawaja, N. G., White, K. M., Schweitzer, R., & Greenslade, J. H. (2008). Difficulties and coping strategies of Sudanese refugees: A qualitative approach. *Transcultural Psychiatry, 45*(3), 489–512.

Khawaja, N. G., & Milner, K. (2012). Acculturation stress in South Sudanese refugees: Impact on marital relationships. *International Journal of Intercultural Relations, 36*(5), 624–636. https://doi.org/10.1016/j.ijintrel.2012.03.007

Klarić, M., Francisković, T., Klarić, B., et al. (2008). Social support and PTSD symptoms in war-traumatized women in Bosnia and Herzegovina. *Psychiatria Danubina, 20*, 466–473.

Lee, R. M., & Liu, H.-T. T. (2001). Coping with intergenerational family conflict: Comparison of Asian American, Hispanic, and European American college students. *Journal of Counseling Psychology, 48*(4), 410–419. https://doi.org/10.1037/0022-0167.48.4.410

Mähönen, T. A., & Jasinskaja-Lahti, I. (2013). Acculturation expectations and experiences as predictors of ethnic migrants' psychological well-being. *Journal of Cross-Cultural Psychology, 44*(5), 786–806. https://doi.org/10.1177/0022022112466699

Marlowe, J., Harris, A., & Lyons, T. (Eds.). (2014). *South Sudanese diaspora in Australia and New Zealand: Reconciling the past with the present*. Cambridge Scholars Publishing.

Marvasti, J. A. (2012). War Trauma in Veterans and Their Families: Diagnosis and Management of PTSD, TBI and Comorbidities of Combat Trauma: From Pharmacotherapy to a 12-Step Self-Help Program for Combat Veterans.

Milner, K., & Khawaja, N. G. (2010). Sudanese Refugees in Australia: The Impact of Acculturation Stress. *Journal of Pacific Rim Psychology, 4*(1), 19–29. https://doi.org/10.1375/prp.4.1.19

Mshweshwe, L. (2020). Understanding domestic violence: Masculinity, culture, traditions. *Heliyon, 6*(10), e05334. https://doi.org/10.1016/j.heliyon.2020.e05334

Muchoki, S. M. (2013). '[In Australia] what comes first are the women, then children, cats, dogs, followed by men': Exploring accounts of gender relations by men from the Horn of Africa. *Australasian Review of African Studies 34*(2), 78–98.

Mungai, N. W., & Gitau, L. W. (2019). African refugee women in Australia: Domestic and family violence experience. In A. Kalunta-Crumpton (Ed.), *Violence against women of African descent: Global perspectives* (1st ed., pp. 211–228). Lexington Books.

Ndhlovu, F. (2014). *Becoming an African Diaspora in Australia: Language, Culture, Identity*. London: Palgrave Macmillan.

Olff, M., Hein, I., Amstadter, A. B., Armour, C., Skogbrott Birkeland, M., Bui, E., Cloitre, M., Ehlers, A., Ford, J. D., Greene, T., Hansen, M., Harnett, N. G., Kaminer, D., Lewis, C., Minelli, A., Niles, B., Nugent, N. R., Roberts, N., Price, M., Reffi, A. N., ... Vujanovic, A. A. (2025). The impact of trauma and how to intervene: A narrative review of psychotraumatology over the past 15 years. *European Journal of Psychotraumatology, 16*(1), 2458406. https://doi.org/10.1080/20008066.2025.2458406

Our Watch. (2019). *Men in focus: Unpacking masculinities and engaging men in the prevention of violence against women, Our Watch.* Melbourne, Australia.

Ogunsiji, O., Foster, J., Green, H., Sikhosana, N., Gauci, P., Kayesa, N., & Fernandez, R. (2025). Experiences of African women who migrate to a developed country and encounter intimate partner violence: A systematic review of qualitative evidence. *JBI evidence synthesis,* https://doi.org/10.11124/JBIES-23-00391. Advance online publication. https://doi.org/10.11124/JBIES-23-00391

Pittaway, T., Riggs, E., & Dantas, J. A. R. (2022). Intergenerational conflict among resettled South Sudanese in Australia. *Transcultural Psychiatry,* 13634615221105115. Advance online publication. https://doi.org/10.1177/13634615221105115

Tempany, M. (2009). What research tells us about the mental health and on psychosocial wellbeing of Sudanese refugees: A literature review. *Transcultural Psychiatry, 46*(2), 300–315.

Ramsay, R., Gorst-Unsworth, C., & Turner, S. (1993). Psychiatric morbidity in survivors of organised state violence including torture. A retrospective series. *The British Journal of Psychiatry: The Journal of Mental Science, 162,* 55–59. https://doi.org/10.1192/bjp.162.1.55

Redfield, R., Linton, R., & Herskovits, M. (1936). Memorandum for Acculturation. *American Anthropologist, 38,* 149–152. https://doi.org/10.1525/aa.1936.38.1.02a00330

Robinson, S., & valentine, k., Newton, B. J., Smyth, C., & Parmenter, N. (2020). *Violence prevention and early intervention for mothers and children with disability: Building promising practice (Research report, 16/2020).* ANROWS.

Schweitzer, R., Melville, F., Steel, Z., & Lacherez, P. (2006). Trauma, post-migration living difficulties, and social support as predictors of psychological adjustment in resettled Sudanese refugees. *Australian and New Zealand Journal of Psychiatry, 40*(2), 179–187.

Spangaro, J., Spence, N., Cameron, J., Hegarty, K., Koziol-McLain, J., Man, N. et al. (2024). *Domestic violence identification and response for refugee women in settlement services* (The SAHAR Study). University of Wollongong. Report. https://hdl.handle.net/10779/uow.27779094.v1

Sylvester, C. (1995). African and Western Feminisms: World-Traveling the Tendencies and Possibilities. *Signs, 20*(4), 941–969. http://www.jstor.org/stable/3174888

van der Kolk, B. A., Roth, S., Pelcovitz, D., Sunday, S., & Spinazzola, J. (2005). Disorders of extreme stress: The empirical foundation of a complex adaptation to trauma. *Journal of Traumatic Stress, 18*(5), 389–399. https://doi.org/10.1002/jts.20047

Victorian Government. (2021). Data collection standards—Culturally and linguistically diverse communities. www.vic.gov.au. https://www.vic.gov.au/victorian-family-violence-data collection-framework/data-collectionstandards-culturally

Ward, C. (2001). The A, B, Cs of Acculturation. In D. Matsumoto (Ed.), *The handbook of culture and psychology* (pp. 411–445). Oxford University Press.

Webster, K., Diemer, K., Honey, N., Mannix, S., Mickle, J., Morgan, J., Parkes, A., Politoff, V., Powell, A., Stubbs, J., & Ward, A. (2018). *Australians' attitudes to violence against women and gender equality. Findings from the 2017 National Community Attitudes towards Violence against Women Survey (NCAS)* (Research report, 03/2018). ANROWS.

Yakeley, J. (2018). Psychoanalysis in modern mental health practice. The lancet. *Psychiatry, 5*(5), 443–450. https://doi.org/10.1016/S2215-0366(18)30052-X

4

African Customary Law and Family Violence

Introduction

Chapter 3 presented and analysed empirical findings on the factors contributing to family violence experiences within the South Sudanese community. Therefore, it is important to follow this with a discussion of how family violence is or was traditionally addressed within African communities, particularly South Sudanese approaches, followed by a discussion in Chapter 5 on how family violence is addressed in Australia through the family law system. This chapter also explores the disparities between the two systems in their approaches to family violence intervention and prevention. These discussions help ground the upcoming chapters, which continue to present empirical findings.

In many African countries, including South Sudan, customary law is not only recognised but also enshrined in their constitutions, functioning as a parallel legal system to statutory law (Diala & Kangwa, 2019). Customary law in Africa governs vital aspects of social life, particularly in relation to marriage, inheritance, family disputes—including family violence—and dispute resolution (Diala & Kangwa, 2019). What makes African customary law distinct is its deeply communal nature, reflecting the values, traditions, and historical experiences of diverse ethnic groups

A. K. Anyieth, *Decolonising Family Violence Legal Intervention Orders in African-Australian Communities*, https://doi.org/10.1007/978-3-031-95404-7_4

across the continent (Himonga & Bosch, 2000; Perera, 2024). However, as mentioned in Chapter 2, African countries are not homogeneous; each nation possesses its own unique set of customary legal traditions. Nevertheless, there are striking similarities that run through different societies (Perera, 2024). These shared values shape how families function, how disputes are settled, and how social order is maintained. Among the crucial issues governed by customary law is the resolution of family disputes, including cases of family violence, which is the focus of this chapter. The way customary law addresses family violence varies across cultures, but it generally emphasises reconciliation, community mediation, and restorative justice over punitive measures (Himonga & Bosch, 2000).

First, this chapter delves into how customary law has historically functioned as a mechanism for addressing family disputes, particularly before and after colonial rule. It explores the ways in which African societies traditionally handled domestic conflicts and how the imposition of statutory laws during colonial rule altered these mechanisms. Furthermore, it considers the post-colonial evolution of customary law, analysing the ongoing intersection between traditional legal norms and modern human rights discourses as they relate to family violence intervention. Ultimately, this chapter aims to provide a nuanced understanding of how customary law continues to shape family life in Africa and among Africans in the diaspora, particularly in Australia, as well as the challenges it faces in addressing contemporary issues such as gender equality and victim protection in cases of family violence. The chapter also compares African customary law with Indigenous customary law and practices in Western countries such as Australia, New Zealand, the United States, and Canada. Finally, it presents arguments against the applicability of customary law in modern-day family disputes, particularly in cases of family violence, as well as arguments in favour of its relevance.

The chapter concludes by restating its main argument in relation to the decolonisation of Family Violence Intervention Orders (FVIOs) within African Australian communities and provides a brief overview of the upcoming chapter.

Customary Law in Pre-colonial Africa

Part of this book emphasises a decolonial approach to explore how family issues, particularly family violence and its resolution, were traditionally addressed in African contexts before and after migration to Australia. Understanding these practices is essential to fully grasp how African Australians, especially South Sudanese communities, navigate family disputes within Australia's legal system. Without acknowledging these influences, any attempt to address family violence within these communities' risks being ineffective and disconnected from their lived realities.

Customary law in pre-colonial Africa was a dynamic and evolving system of norms rather than a rigid or codified set of legal rules (Ndulo, 2011). Unlike modern legal systems, which rely on written statutes and formal court structures, customary law was largely unwritten and transmitted orally across generations (Perera, 2024). Its legitimacy was deeply rooted in long-standing traditions and collective societal values, ensuring that legal principles could adapt to social changes over time (Bennett, 2011). In many African societies, customary law coexisted with religious and colonial legal traditions, resulting in legal pluralism, where Indigenous, statutory, and religious laws intersected—sometimes complementing each other and at other times leading to conflicts (Faris, 2015). African customary law shaped governance structures across the continent, particularly in marriage, inheritance, and dispute resolution. Unlike statutory laws, which are often rigid, customary law remained fluid and adaptable, allowing communities to uphold their cultural identity while responding to evolving societal needs (Bennett, 2011). Enforced by elders, chiefs, and traditional councils, it prioritised reconciliation, family unity, forgiveness, and communal harmony over punitive measures (Faris, 2015).

One of the fundamental characteristics of African customary law was its emphasis on communal justice and social harmony, which shaped how conflicts were resolved within traditional societies (Bennett, 2011; Sinitsina, 1987). Unlike Western legal traditions, which prioritise individual rights, adversarial litigation, and punitive justice, African customary law was rooted in collective responsibility and reconciliation (Sinitsina, 1987). Justice was not merely a means of punishment but a mechanism for restoring balance within the family and the wider community, ensuring that disputes were settled in a way that reinforced social cohesion and stability.

This community-oriented approach meant that justice systems were designed to prevent the escalation of conflicts by resolving them at the earliest possible stage through mediation and negotiated settlements rather than legal retribution (Engle Merry, 1988). The primary objective was to ensure that both the victim and the offender could continue to coexist peacefully within the same community, preventing long-term hostility or exclusion. This philosophy was particularly significant in family disputes, where elders and community leaders played a pivotal role in dispute resolution, guiding individuals towards reconciliation rather than separation (Sippel, 1998). Furthermore, in many African societies, punitive justice was viewed as a last resort because of its potential to fracture social ties and weaken communal bonds (Bennett, 2011). Instead, restorative justice mechanisms such as apology, restitution, and community service were employed to repair damaged relationships and reintegrate offenders (Sippel, 1998). By prioritising dialogue and collective accountability, African customary law ensured that justice was not merely about penalising wrongdoers but about rebuilding trust and preserving long-term social order (Fenrich et al., 2011).

Fadlalla (2009) argue that the enforcement of customary law was not carried out by formal legal institutions but rather by community elders, chiefs, and family heads, who were the custodians of Indigenous legal traditions. These figures held deep knowledge of customs, moral expectations, and cultural values, making them the primary mediators in conflict resolution, including disputes between intimate partners and family members (Fenrich et al., 2011). Their authority was widely recognised and respected by all members of the community, as they were considered the guardians of justice and tradition. Unlike modern legal interventions, which rely on police, courts, and judicial systems, customary law functioned through collective social enforcement, ensuring that justice was administered in a way that preserved communal bonds and reinforced shared moral values (Fadlalla, 2009).

The primary goal of customary law was not simply to enforce rules but to reinforce social cohesion and stability, ensuring that conflicts were resolved in a way that strengthened relationships rather than severing them. This was particularly important in societies where kinship ties and extended family structures played a central role in governance and collective survival (Behrendt, 2003). However, this does not mean that offenders went unpunished. In many cases, wrongdoers were required to compensate victims and comply with other forms of punishment imposed by elders, family, or community heads (Fadlalla, 2009). These forms of punishment focused on restoring balance and repairing social fractures, thereby preventing future conflicts from escalating.

In many African societies, maintaining family and social unity was considered more important than addressing individual grievances, as the well-being of the community was deeply interwoven with the stability of family structures (Sinitsina, 1987). The belief that an individual's actions could affect the entire family and community meant that disputes were not private matters but communal concerns. This perspective encouraged mediation and reconciliation, as prolonged conflicts could weaken family alliances, disrupt social harmony, and negatively impact collective welfare (Sinitsina, 1987). By resolving conflicts through customary processes, communities ensured that relationships were preserved and that families remained functional even after disputes. The use of customary law in family matters was vital in pre-colonial African societies because it was deeply embedded within the cultural, spiritual, and communal fabric of life, serving not only as a legal framework but as a mechanism for social cohesion and moral order. Customary law reflected the lived realities, values, and worldviews of African communities, emphasising restorative justice, collective responsibility, and the centrality of kinship networks in resolving disputes. In family matters—such as marriage, inheritance, child-rearing, and conflict resolution—customary practices ensured that decisions were made with regard to social harmony, lineage obligations, and the preservation of community identity. Unlike colonial legal systems that privileged individual rights and formal procedures, African customary law was oral, flexible, and consensus-driven, evolving through community deliberation and guided by elders and traditional leaders. Its importance lay not only in its responsiveness to local norms and practices but also in its role in maintaining balance and continuity within African societies long before the imposition of colonial rule.

The emphasis on reconciliation over punishment meant that wrongdoers were often encouraged to make amends through negotiation, apology, and restitution rather than being ostracised (Sinitsina, 1987). Customary justice systems viewed wrongdoing not as an individual moral failure but as a social issue that required collective intervention. This was particularly evident in family affairs, marriage, inheritance, and domestic disputes, including cases of family violence (Sippel, 1998). Rather than punishing offenders through imprisonment or exile, traditional leaders sought solutions that ensured offenders could reintegrate into society, often requiring public apologies, fines, or acts of restitution to restore harmony.

Although this system effectively maintained social unity, critics argue that it sometimes placed undue pressure on victims to forgive and reconcile, especially in cases of domestic violence and gender-based abuse (Fadlalla, 2009). This tension between preserving communal harmony and protecting individual rights highlights the ongoing need for harmonisation between customary dispute resolution and modern statutory legal protections. In communities where customary practices remain influential but are not recognised by statutory legal systems, bridging this gap remains an important legal and social challenge (Fadlalla, 2009).

Family Structures and Gender Roles in Pre-Colonial African Societies

In pre-colonial Africa, family structure and gender roles played a crucial role in the coexistence and stability of individuals, families, and communities. They served as the primary social institutions through which responsibilities, identities, and moral values were transmitted. The extended family system served as the foundation of social organisation, providing economic support, caregiving, conflict resolution, and social protection. While patriarchal norms often influenced gender roles, they were not static or universally hierarchical; instead, they were deeply contextual and typically complementary. Women and men held distinct yet interdependent and equally important responsibilities that contributed to the well-being of the community. For instance, men were generally tasked with external affairs such as warfare and diplomacy, while women played crucial roles in agriculture, market economies, spiritual life, and the transmission of cultural knowledge. one role was not more important than other but complement each other while serving the overall vision of the family and society. These structured roles established a clear social order, ensuring intergenerational continuity that reinforced the collective ethos and mutual obligations vital for survival, cooperation, and cohesion in African societies before colonial disruptions. Many of these traditions and practices continue to coexist with colonial influences and modern ways of life in various parts of Africa today. Family structures in pre-colonial Africa were deeply influenced by kinship networks, which played a vital role in economic, social, and legal affairs (Mbembe & Ginsburg, 2021). Unlike the nuclear family model that dominates Western societies, African families were predominantly extended, consisting of multiple generations living together (Awusabo-Asare, 1990). The extended family was considered the basic unit of society, and decision-making was collective, involving elders, parents, and other influential relatives (Greene, 1999). These extended family networks provided social security for individuals, as wealth and resources were shared among relatives (Greene, 1999). In times of crisis, such as family disputes, marriage conflicts, or domestic violence, the extended family played a crucial role in mediating tensions and ensuring that the well-being of all members was prioritised (Bennett, 2011). However, this safety net provided by kinship and family has significantly diminished, particularly for African families in Australia, where community and family structures are more individual-based and primarily governed by national and state laws.

Customary Dispute Resolution: Addressing Family Violence

One of the defining features of African customary law is its approach to conflict resolution, which emphasises mediation, dialogue, and reconciliation over punitive justice (Awusabo-Asare, 1990; Bennett, 2011). This principle is particularly evident in cases of family violence, where such incidents are not viewed as isolated conflicts between individuals but rather as matters affecting the broader family and community (Tamale, 2020). In many African societies, maintaining harmony within the family and preserving social cohesion is prioritised over legal punishment, making customary dispute resolution a cornerstone of justice administration.

Unlike Western legal frameworks, where domestic violence cases are handled by state institutions through criminal prosecution, customary legal systems involve family elders, chiefs, and traditional councils as mediators (Tamale, 2020). These figures intervene to restore balance between conflicting parties rather than imposing legal penalties that could potentially sever relationships (Chanock, 1985). Given that family and kinship structures play a central role in African societies, resolving disputes through customary means was considered a more effective and culturally appropriate method of addressing issues related to marriage, domestic conflicts, and inheritance disputes (Bennett, 2011). However, while this approach promotes reconciliation and community healing, it has been criticised (expanded discussion of these critiques towards the end of the chapter) for failing to provide adequate protection for victims of family violence, particularly women and children.

Elders and Family Heads as Mediators

In pre-colonial African societies, and even today in some communities, cases of family conflict or family violence were first addressed through mediation by family elders (Bennett, 2011). Rather than turning to external authorities or formal courts for legal interventions such as Family Violence Intervention Orders (FVIOs), the extended family and community leaders would intervene between the conflicting parties (Fadlalla, 2009). The mediation process was structured to ensure that both the victim and the offender were heard, with the resolution upholding the dignity and interests of all parties involved (Tamale, 2014). Unlike the FVIO system, where a perpetrator is issued with an intervention order document and, in some cases, removed from the property where the victim resides, the customary dispute resolution process typically involved several key stages before removal of the perpetrator.

Listening to Grievances

The first step in mediation was allowing both parties to present their grievances before a council of elders or family representatives (Sibanda, 2020). This stage was highly structured and ritualistic, as speaking in the presence of elders was regarded as a solemn and significant act. The accused party was also given an opportunity to defend themselves or explain their actions, ensuring that both sides of the dispute were fairly represented (Chanock, 1985). In some societies, the wider community, including extended relatives and neighbours, would also be invited to observe the proceedings. This reinforced the idea that the dispute affected not just the individuals involved but the broader social structure, while also triggering a sense of shame in the perpetrator for the crime they had committed (Stewart, 2018).

However, while the Australian legal system is based on an adversarial approach that considers accounts from both sides, the intervention order system allows the police to issue an interim order or intervene in the respondent's absence if they fail to appear in court on the designated day. Although this measure is intended to protect the victim, it can leave absent respondents—or those who do not fully understand the rushed legal process (as discussed in the following chapter)—at risk of breaching the order. When FVIOs are issued without a clear explanation of what is required, individuals may inadvertently violate the terms. In some cases, the disregard for their account of the incident, coupled with a lack of understanding, can lead to further aggravation, potentially putting the applicant at greater risk of escalating violence.

Encouraging Dialogue and Seeking Resolution

According to customary practices, once grievances had been expressed, mediators guided discussions to identify the root causes of the conflict and explore possible solutions (Bennett, 2011). In cases of family violence, elders would typically ask probing questions to determine whether external factors—such as financial stress, infertility, misunderstandings, or influence from extended relatives—had contributed to the situation (Nhlapo, 2017). The use of elders in resolving family violence cases has also been shown to be effective in Indigenous Australian communities (see Blagg et al., 2022). The discussion would then focus on restoring peace, with emphasis placed on forgiveness, mutual understanding, and behavioural reform (Sibanda, 2020). Unlike modern courts, where verdicts are imposed by judges, customary mediators encouraged both parties to voluntarily agree on a fair resolution, reinforcing the idea that justice should be collaborative rather than coercive (Moyo, 2013).

Restitution and Compensation

If harm had been caused, particularly in cases of domestic violence or marital disputes, the offender was often required to offer compensation—such as livestock, money, or gifts—to the aggrieved party as a form of restorative justice (Sibanda, 2020). These compensations were not forced upon the victim but were only pursued if the victim accepted the approach. This practice, common in many African communities, was not merely a financial transaction or an alternative to serving time in prison but rather a symbolic gesture of atonement and reconciliation (Stewart, 2018). Compensation was intended to restore dignity to the victim, provide economic support, and reinforce the offender's responsibility to reform their behaviour (Bennett, 2011). The involvement of family members in overseeing restitution also served as a deterrent, discouraging further violence by emphasising the collective responsibility of the community in upholding justice (Moyo, 2013).

Ensuring Long-Term Harmony

In contrast to the Australian Family Violence Intervention Order (FVIO) system, which has an expiration date—short-term orders lasting six months and long-term orders lasting up to five years, subject to renewal by the victim and based on the court's assessment of the risk of continued violence—African customary practice extends beyond a fixed compensation timeline. It allows elders to monitor the behaviour of both parties to ensure that the resolution is effective and lasting. In cases of repeat offences, mediators could impose stricter measures, such as a more significant compensation payment, temporary separation—whereby the offender is placed in the care of another, usually an elder relative—or, in extreme cases, the dissolution of the marriage (Bennett, 2011). The goal was to prevent the recurrence of violence while preserving social order, ensuring that families remained functional and community bonds remained intact.

Comparisons: Customary Laws Outside Africa

African customary law is not the only legal system that prioritises mediation and reconciliation over punitive justice. Indigenous communities, such as those studied by Blagg et al. (2022), and others in different parts of the world share similar approaches to dispute resolution. However, there are also notable differences in how these customs have evolved in response to modern legal systems.

Indigenous Legal Traditions in Australia and New Zealand

Among Aboriginal Australians and the Māori of New Zealand, traditional dispute resolution systems place a strong emphasis on recognising the harmful legacies of colonialism and systemic structures that continue to disadvantage Indigenous communities (Cunneen et al., 2023). They also prioritise community involvement in approaches to family violence intervention and prevention, as well as reconciliation and restorative justice. Much like African customary law, these Indigenous legal traditions prioritise healing relationships over punitive measures (Atkinson, 1990). The goal is to restore social harmony and reintegrate offenders into the community rather than isolate them through imprisonment (Sasmiar et al., 2024). This communal approach reflects a deep-rooted belief in collective responsibility for repair and the importance of preserving social cohesion within Indigenous societies.

However, a key distinction between African and Australasian customary legal systems lies in their formal legal recognition. In many African nations, customary law continues to be widely practised and constitutionally recognised, often coexisting alongside statutory legal frameworks. In contrast, Indigenous law in Australia and New Zealand operates under more limited recognition. While the Māori Rangatiratanga (chieftainship) system has been partially integrated into New Zealand's legal framework, allowing for some degree of self-governance, Aboriginal customary law in Australia largely functions informally, particularly in rural areas, with many community leaders and elders advocating for formal recognition (Anthony & Blagg, 2013).

Native American Legal Traditions in the United States and Canada

Despite their historical significance, Native American legal traditions have been significantly weakened by colonial intervention. Over the centuries, colonial and federal governments imposed strict legal frameworks that eroded the authority of Indigenous legal systems. Although tribal courts still exist, they operate under strict limitations imposed by national laws, particularly in the United States and Canada (Das, Veena and Others, 2021). In many cases, these courts are restricted in their ability to handle serious legal matters, leading to gaps in justice for Indigenous communities.

These shared colonial legacies—characterised by violence, the erasure of cultural practices, and the imposition of colonial approaches to dispute resolution—have had lasting effects on Indigenous communities in North America, as well as African communities in Australia. As a result, these communities have been left vulnerable to high rates of family violence, with some experiencing higher rates than others. However, the key issue remains that sidelining customary approaches to family violence intervention and prevention has, in many cases, exacerbated the problem rather than provided effective solutions.

The Divide on the Usefulness of Customary Law in Family Violence Matters

The application of customary law in addressing family disputes, particularly cases involving family violence, has been the subject of considerable scholarly debate, which I acknowledge. Broadly, scholars are divided into two distinct camps: one that advocates for the use of customary law in family dispute resolution with an optimistic outlook and another that critically opposes its application, arguing that it perpetuates patriarchal structures and violates fundamental human rights. While both perspectives offer valid critiques and insights, I propose a more balanced, pragmatic approach—one that recognises the potential of customary law while also addressing its limitations in the context of family violence intervention and prevention.

However, before outlining this perspective, it is important to briefly discuss the ongoing debate regarding the role and relevance of customary law in contemporary African families, both on the continent and in the diaspora. These two opposing viewpoints—often described as 'customary law romanticists' and 'critical legal theorists'—represent two sides of the same coin.

Despite its strengths in maintaining social cohesion, as argued above, customary law has faced significant challenges, particularly in areas of gender equality and the rights of vulnerable groups. Patriarchal structures have historically influenced legal interpretations, often disadvantaging women and children in family disputes. These complexities, along with ongoing legal reforms and human rights advocacy, continue to shape contemporary discussions on the role of customary law in Africa and its relevance for African communities today.

Customary Law: A Means of Oppressing Women

Scholars such as Ezer (2016) adopt a highly critical stance towards the application of customary law in family disputes, arguing that "customary law is used to promote patriarchy and disempower women" (Ezer, 2016, p. 66). Bavinck (2013), Ezer (2016) and Ndulo, (2018) argue that customary law often serves as an instrument of patriarchal control, reinforcing gender hierarchies that disadvantage women. From this perspective, customary legal frameworks tend to prioritise male authority, uphold discriminatory practices, and perpetuate the normalisation of domestic violence under the guise of cultural tradition.

One of the primary critiques is that customary law often lacks robust protections for women's rights. In many traditional societies, cultural norms that emphasise obedience, family honour, and female subordination to male relatives may discourage women from seeking redress for family violence. In some cases, customary legal processes may even mandate reconciliation between victims and perpetrators, thereby silencing women and preventing them from accessing justice (Ezer, 2016). Ezer (2016) argues that such practices not only violate international human rights standards but also entrench cycles of abuse and impunity.

Moreover, this group contends that customary law is inherently incompatible with contemporary human rights principles. They argue that reliance on customary legal mechanisms in cases of family violence may undermine efforts to combat gender-based violence and promote gender equality. Given these concerns, critical scholars advocate for the primacy of formal legal frameworks, which they believe offer stronger legal protections, enforceable rights, and impartial adjudication processes that are less susceptible to patriarchal biases.

However, while these critiques highlight significant concerns about the potential for customary law to reinforce gender oppression, the pessimistic outlook of these scholars' risks dismissing the potential benefits of customary dispute resolution mechanisms. The outright rejection of customary law may also alienate communities that view such legal traditions as integral to their cultural identity, thereby hindering meaningful legal reform and engagement. A more balanced approach is necessary—one that critically examines the limitations of customary law while also recognising its role in promoting community cohesion and accessible justice.

Customary Law: A Tool for Preserving African Culture, Traditions, and Practices

A segment of scholars maintains an optimistic perspective regarding the application of customary law in family disputes. Scholars such as Atkinson (1990, 2011), Sébastien Grammond (2013), Ozoemena (2014), Himonga and Diallo (2017), and Blagg et al. (2022), among others, emphasise the cultural significance, historical continuity, and community-based mechanisms inherent in customary legal frameworks. They argue that customary law is deeply rooted in Indigenous and local traditions, reflecting the values and social structures of the communities it governs. As such, they contend that it remains an effective mechanism for resolving family disputes, including those involving violence.

One of the key arguments put forth by these scholars is that customary law fosters restorative justice, reconciliation, and communal harmony—principles that colonial legal systems have historically sought to erode. Unlike formal legal frameworks that often prioritise punitive measures, customary law emphasises mediation, consensus-building, and the intervention of community elders. This approach is believed to provide culturally relevant solutions that disputing parties are more likely to accept and adhere to.

Moreover, proponents argue that customary law is more accessible to marginalised populations, particularly those in rural or Indigenous communities, where state legal institutions may be distant, expensive, or culturally alien. By offering community-driven resolutions that align with local traditions, customary law is seen as a more inclusive and practical means of addressing family disputes, ensuring justice is both meaningful and attainable for those who rely on it.

A Practical Approach: Integrating Customary Law with Modern Legal Frameworks

Rather than adopting an overly optimistic or entirely dismissive stance, I propose a pragmatic and context-specific approach that integrates elements of customary law with modern legal frameworks to effectively address family violence. A realistic perspective acknowledges both the strengths and limitations of customary law, aiming to reform and adapt traditional dispute resolution mechanisms while ensuring they align with human rights principles and cultural standards.

One potential solution is the establishment of hybrid dispute resolution mechanisms that incorporate customary legal principles while adhering to state and international human rights laws (this hybrid approach to addressing family violence in African Australian communities is discussed in detail in the conclusion chapter). For instance, community-based mediation could be supplemented with legal protections to ensure that women's voices are heard and their rights upheld. Additionally, training community elders and customary law practitioners in gender sensitivity and human rights norms could help mitigate the patriarchal biases often present in traditional dispute resolution systems.

Furthermore, legal pluralism—the coexistence of multiple legal systems within a society—can be leveraged to create more inclusive and effective frameworks for addressing family violence. Governments and legal institutions should collaborate with customary law practitioners to ensure that victims of family violence have access to multiple avenues for justice, including both customary dispute resolution and formal legal proceedings.

Ultimately, the goal is not to uncritically accept or reject customary law practices but to refine and modernise them in ways that protect vulnerable populations while preserving their culturally significant dispute resolution mechanisms. By adopting a reform-oriented approach, customary law can be harnessed as a tool for addressing family violence in a manner that is both culturally relevant and aligned with principles of justice and human rights.

Conclusion

This chapter has provided an in-depth exploration of African customary law and its role in addressing family violence, tracing its historical roots, colonial disruptions, and ongoing evolution in post-colonial societies. The discussion has highlighted the unique characteristics of customary legal systems, particularly their emphasis on community mediation, reconciliation, and the preservation of family unity. Unlike Western legal frameworks, which prioritise punitive justice, African customary law focuses on restoring social harmony—an approach that, while valuable, also presents significant challenges in ensuring justice and protection for victims of family violence.

One of the core arguments of this chapter is that while customary law remains a vital legal and cultural institution, it must evolve to align with modern human rights standards and statutory legal protections. The chapter has examined gender biases, patriarchal structures, and inadequate victim protection, all of which continue to limit the effectiveness of customary dispute resolution in cases of domestic violence. Additionally, the legal pluralism that characterises many African legal systems—where customary and statutory law coexist—has created both opportunities and tensions, necessitating careful harmonisation to ensure that justice is not compromised for the sake of tradition.

Despite these challenges, customary law remains deeply embedded in African societies, providing accessible and culturally relevant means of dispute resolution. It continues to serve as the primary legal framework for many individuals, particularly in rural and traditional communities, where formal legal institutions may be distant or inaccessible. Moreover, customary law plays a crucial role in strengthening communal ties, maintaining social cohesion, and preserving Indigenous African legal traditions.

As African nations modernise their legal systems, there is increasing recognition that customary law should not be discarded but rather reformed and harmonised with statutory legal protections. The integration of statutory safeguards within customary legal mechanisms—such as ensuring gender equality in customary marriage laws and formalising legal protections for victims of family violence with constitutional principles—offers a pathway towards a more balanced and effective legal system.

Ultimately, the future of customary law lies in its ability to adapt to the changing needs of African societies. Legal reforms that preserve the strengths of traditional dispute resolution while ensuring justice, fairness, and individual rights will be essential in maintaining customary law as a relevant and respected component of Africa's legal landscape. By fostering dialogue between traditional leaders, statutory legal institutions, and human rights advocates, African societies can create a legal framework that is both culturally authentic and just—one that protects the most vulnerable while upholding the rich heritage of African customary law.

As Africa navigates its legal evolution, customary law stands as a testament to the continent's rich history, resilience, and adaptability. It remains an essential pillar of African identity and governance but must grow and transform to meet the demands of a modern, rights-based legal system. The future of customary law lies not in its rejection but in its refinement—ensuring that tradition and justice work hand in hand to protect families, individuals, and communities.

References

Anthony, T., Blagg, H. (2013). 'STOP in the name of who's law? Driving and the regulation of contested space in central Australia'. *Social and Legal Studies, 22*(1), 43.

Atkinson, J. (1990). Violence against aboriginal women reconstitution of community law—The way forward. *Aboriginal Law Bulletin, 2*(51), 4–6.

Awusabo-Asare, K. (1990). Matriliny and the new intestate succession law of Ghana. *Canadian Journal of African Studies/Revue canadienne des études africaines, 24*(1), 1–16. https://doi.org/10.1080/00083968.1990.10803849

Bavinck, E. A. (2013). Conflicting priorities? Issues of gender equality in South Africa's customary law. *Amsterdam Law Forum, 5*(2), 20. https://doi.org/10.37974/alf.249

Behrendt, L. (2003). *Indigenous dispute resolution and restorative justice*. The Federation Press.

Bennett, T. W. (2011). *Customary law in South Africa*. Juta.

Blagg, H., Hovane, V., Tulich, T., Raye, D., May, S., & Worrigal, T. (2022). Law, culture and decolonisation: The perspectives of aboriginal elders on family violence in Australia. *Social & Legal Studies, 31*(4), 535–558. https://doi.org/10.1177/09646639211046134.

Chanock, M. (1985). *Law, custom, and social order: The colonial experience in Malawi and Zambia*. Cambridge University Press.

Cunneen, C., Deckert, A., Porter, A., Tauri, J., & Webb, R. (2023). *The Routledge international handbook on decolonizing justice*. Taylor & Francis.

Das, Veena, & others, 'Reimagining Aboriginality: An Indigenous People's Response to Social Suffering', Remaking a World: Violence, Social Suffering, and Recovery (Oakland, CA, 2001; online edn, California Scholarship Online, 24 May 2012), https://doi.org/10.1525/california/9780520223295.003.0003, accessed 4 July 2025.

Diala, A. C., & Kangwa, B. (2019). Rethinking the interface between customary law and constitutionalism in sub-Saharan Africa. *De Jure, 52*(1). https://doi.org/10.17159/2225-7160/2019/v52a12

Engle Merry, S. (1988). Legal pluralism. *Law & Society Review, 22*(5), 869–896. https://doi.org/10.2307/3053638

Ezer, T. (2016). Forging a path for women's rights in customary law. *Hastings Women's Law Journal,* 27(1), 65–86. Available at SSRN: https://ssrn.com/abstract=3936810

Fadlalla, M. (2009). *Customary laws in Southern Sudan*. iUniverse.

Faris, J. A. (2015). African customary law and common law in South Africa: Reconciling contending legal systems. *International Journal of African Renaissance Studies - Multi-, Inter- and Transdisciplinarity, 10*(2), 171–189. https://doi.org/10.1080/18186874.2015.1107991

Fenrich, J., Galizzi, P., & Higgins, T. E. (2011). *The future of African customary law*. Cambridge University Press

Greene, S. E. (1999). Family concerns: Gender and ethnicity in pre-colonial West Africa. *International Review of Social History, 44*(S7), 15–31. https://doi.org/10.1017/s0020859000115172

Himonga, C., & Diallo, F. (2017). Decolonisation and Teaching Law in Africa with Special Reference to Living Customary Law. *Potchefstroom Electronic*

Law Journal/Potchefstroomse Elektroniese Regsblad, 20, 1. https://doi.org/10.17159/1727-3781/2017/v20i0a3267

Himonga, C., & Bosch, C. (2000). The application of African customary law under the constitution of South Africa: Problems solved or just beginning. *South African Law Journal, 117*(2), 306–341.

Mbembe, A., & Ginsburg, D. (2021). *Out of the dark night: Essays on decolonization*. Columbia University Press.

Moyo, A. (2013). Customary law and family dispute resolution in Africa. *Journal of African Law, 13*(2), 123–140.

Ndulo, M. (2011). African customary law, customs, and women's rights. *Indiana Journal of Global Legal Studies, 18*(1), 87–120. https://doi.org/10.2979/indjglolegstu.18.1.87

Ndulo, M. B. (2018). Legal pluralism, customary law and women's rights. *Southern African Public Law, 32*(1–2), 21. https://doi.org/10.25159/2522-6800/3576

Nhlapo, T. (2017). Customary law in post-apartheid South Africa: constitutional confrontations in culture, gender and 'living law.' *South African Journal on Human Rights, 33*(1), 1–24. https://doi.org/10.1080/02587203.2017.1303900

Ozoemena, R. N. (2014). "Living Customary Law: A Truly Transformative Tool?" Constitutional Court Review 8 [CCR]. 147–163.

Perera, J. (2024). Customs into customary law: Marriage and succession in Kandyan customary law—An anthropological review. *Qeios*. https://doi.org/10.32388/sj3gwb.2

Sasmiar, S., Hasan, U. & Suhermi, S. (2024). LEGAL CERTAINTY OF ALTERNATIVE DISPUTE RESOLUTION MEDIATION. *Bengkoelen Justice: Jurnal Ilmu Hukum, 14*(1), 25–44. https://doi.org/10.33369/jbengkoelenjust.v14i1.33432

Sébastien, G., (2013). *Terms of coexistence : Indigenous peoples and Canadian law*. Toronto, Ontario: Carswell.

Sibanda, O. (2020). Raw life, new hope: Decency, housing and everyday life in a post-apartheid community. *Anthropology Southern Africa, 43*(4), 270–272. https://doi.org/10.1080/23323256.2020.1857276

Sinitsina, I. (1987). African legal tradition J. M. Sarbah, J. B. Danquah, N. A. Ollennu. *Journal of African Law, 31*(1–2), 44–57. https://doi.org/10.1017/S0021855300009232

Sippel, H. (1998). Customary family law in colonial Tanganyika: A study of change and continuity. *Comparative and International Law Journal of Southern Africa, 31*(3), 373–383.

Stewart, J. (2018). *African legal traditions in the modern era*. Cambridge University Press.
Tamale, S. (2014). *African sexualities: A reader*. Pambazuka Press.
Tamale, S. (2020). *Decolonization and Afro-feminism*. Daraja Press.

5

Australian Family Law and Family Violence

Introduction

Chapter 4 provided an overview of African customary law practices, both pre- and post-colonisation, and their role in managing community and family disputes, including family violence. It offered a brief discussion on the evolution of certain African customs and cultures, both on the continent and in their new home countries, such as Australia. This discussion is crucial in examining the changes that many African customs and cultures have undergone—both before and after colonisation—changes that continue to shape their way of life in countries like Australia. This provides essential context for this chapter, which explores Australian family law. Particularly in relation to communities that continue to apply their customary law approaches in the intervention and prevention of family violence and who may come into conflict with the formal family law system in such matters.

Following Chapter 4, it is important to discuss how family-related issues in Australia, such as family violence, are addressed within the Australian family law system. This discussion should highlight the system's progression from its English origins to its application in today's multicultural Australia. This chapter provides a brief historical overview

A. K. Anyieth, *Decolonising Family Violence Legal Intervention Orders in African-Australian Communities*, https://doi.org/10.1007/978-3-031-95404-7_5

of major changes in Australian family law and examines its progress in protecting individuals from family violence. It focuses on the legal safeguards available to victim-survivors and explores published research on the experiences, challenges, and opportunities faced by African families when resolving family disputes, including family violence, within the Australian legal system. The chapter also analyses how Australian law protects victims, holds perpetrators accountable, and considers whether it operates within a framework of legal pluralism.

While this chapter provides essential background for the following chapters—which present empirical analysis of South Sudanese experiences of family violence in Australia—it also makes a significant contribution. There have been numerous amendments to the *Family Law Act 1975*, including recent changes recognising same-sex marriage. However, little attention has been given to the existence of legal pluralism in relation to cultural practices beyond gender and sexuality within Australia. This includes the ways in which African migrant and refugee families, such as the South Sudanese, navigate both formal and customary legal systems when attempting to resolve family violence issues.

Australia Commonwealth Law

Like many African countries with British colonial influences, the legal system introduced to Australia during colonisation did not recognise Aboriginal laws, community structures, or practices, particularly those related to land and family (Hunter, 2003). Indigenous people were subjected to colonial laws and the general law of Australia. The entire continent was treated as terra nullius, meaning "nobody's land", which allowed it to be claimed by the Crown and taken over by the colonisers (Cranwell, 2001).

Common law

The modern Australian legal system shares a history with the English legal system, tracing its origins back nearly 1,000 years to the Norman

Conquest of England in 1066 (Boyle, 2015). It began to develop with the arrival of the first British settlers at Sydney Cove in January 1788, while English institutions continued to play a significant role (Williams, 2005). As a result, Australian law still incorporates many legal principles and doctrines from England and other Commonwealth nations that practise common law. Although English legal thought has significantly influenced Australian lawyers, common law in Australia has evolved based on its own unique experiences (Williams, 2005). While the legal system of eighteenth-century England may be considered Australia's legal foundation, the common law of twenty-first-century Australia is a responsibility that Australians must uphold.

Marriage and Divorce in Australia After the 1900s

In 1788, the British Empire established Australia as a penal colony (Ashkanasy et al., 2002). When convicts arrived on the land of the First Nations People in Australia soon after, few husbands and wives were able to follow their spouses from the United Kingdom to Australia (Ashkanasy et al., 2002).

Despite the First Nations People of Australia having their own laws and governance structures, Australia and other British colonies were able to ratify their own legislation after the British Parliament passed the English Divorce Act in 1857 (Juuk, 2023). The Tasmanian Legislative Council introduced a Divorce Act in 1858, though it was opposed on moral grounds (Juuk, 2023). A subsequent attempt in 1860 was successful, shifting the focus of family law away from protecting the rights of men towards safeguarding wives and children from husbands who had deserted their families (Finlay et al., 1997). This shift is also evident in subsequent legislation.

Australia gained independence in 1901. From 1901 until 1959, marriage and divorce were regulated by the states (Barwick, 1980). The implementation of the Matrimonial Causes Act (1959) and the Commonwealth Marriage Act (1961) brought marriage and divorce under federal jurisdiction (Barwick, 1980).

The Matrimonial Causes Act 1959 introduced "fault-based divorce". To obtain a divorce, a spouse had to prove marital fault. The Act listed reasons for divorce, with the most common being adultery, drunkenness, desertion, habitual imprisonment, and insanity—though it did not mention abuse such as family violence (Barwick, 1962). Private detectives or solicitors were often hired to gather evidence to prove marital fault, making the divorce process costly and time-consuming. Couples were also required to be separated for at least five years before applying for divorce. Additionally, except with leave of the court, a spouse could not apply for a divorce unless the couple had been married for at least three years.

During this era, family law primarily protected the rights of men and gave little consideration to women and children, as they were largely regarded as the man's property. This continued until 1975, when no-fault divorce was introduced. The enactment of the Family Law Act (1975) by the Australian Government is arguably the most significant change in family law in Australia (Jacob, 1989). It marked a dramatic shift in gender relations and significantly advanced the recognition of women's rights. Its most notable impact was the introduction of no-fault divorce (Jacob, 1989). In a no-fault divorce, a spouse no longer had to prove that their partner had done something wrong; instead, they simply had to demonstrate that their relationship had suffered an irretrievable breakdown (Harrison, 2005).

The Family Law Act (1975) also reduced the mandatory separation period for divorce from three years to one month, leading to a surge in divorce cases in 1976 (Harrison, 2005). Despite these legal advancements, the concept of family in Australia still varies significantly among different communities. Many Australians perceive the modern family as the nuclear family—traditionally composed of a man and a woman (with the recent legal recognition of same-sex marriages) living together and raising one or more children to adulthood (Heley & Hewitt, 2022). Historically, the family unit was based on marriage, and family law has largely evolved to protect the traditional nuclear family structure and the institution of marriage.

Conversely, Aboriginal and many other cultural groups regard the family unit as comprising an extended network of individuals related through marriage, blood, adoption, or distant kinships (Rabe & Kumswa, 2022), as discussed in Chapter 1 under the definition of family violence in African communities. Within extended families, members assume designated roles—such as husband, wife, father, mother, son, daughter, brother, sister, uncle, aunt, cousin, or grandparent—and collectively create and maintain a common subculture (Rabe & Kumswa, 2022).

The distinction between nuclear and extended family structures brings diverse perspectives and values regarding legal expectations. Australian family law does not specifically define "family" nor grant it a special legal status—at least not one that is inclusive of multicultural definitions of family. Instead, the law focuses on individual family members and their respective rights and obligations. Australian family law prioritises individual freedom over obligations to family and community. However, despite the lack of an inclusive definition of "family", the law largely assumes the nuclear family as its primary focus (Budinski & Gahan, 2023). In contrast, the majority of ethnic minority communities in Australia emphasise collective values. For them, marriage, divorce, and incidents of family violence are not merely matters concerning individuals but are also of concern to the family, the community, and broader society.

Family and Domestic Violence Under the Family Law Act 1975

This section briefly discusses the inclusion of family violence and dispute resolution in Australia and how African families access or fail to access services to resolve family law problems currently faced in the country. Australia is one of the world's leaders in establishing robust family violence protection and resolution mechanisms.

Prior to the 1970s, the law was reluctant to intervene in cases of family violence because it occurred in private and was considered beyond its jurisdiction. However, during the 1970s and 1980s, there were increasing calls for family violence to be recognised and treated as a crime. These calls influenced policy and justice system reforms in many Western countries, including Australia.

The focus generated by the women's movement during the 1970s led to the establishment of women's shelters, which, in turn, intensified the pressure for legal reform. This movement contributed to the introduction of the *Family Law Act 1975*, which recognises family and domestic violence (Chisholm, 2007). The *Family Law Act 1975* is the primary legislation governing family law in Australia. It includes provisions that recognise family violence and its implications for parenting arrangements and property settlements (Chisholm, 2007).

Although there is no single, uniform family violence act in Australia, each state and territory has its own legislation addressing family and domestic violence, such as the *Domestic Violence Act 2007* (NT), the *Domestic and Family Violence Protection Act 2012* (QLD), the *Family Violence Protection Act 2008* (VIC), and the *Domestic Violence Act 1996* (NSW). These laws provide frameworks for protective orders, police responses, and support services for victims of family and domestic violence. However, the legislation continues to evolve, reflecting changes in societal attitudes towards family violence. Ongoing reforms aim to improve legal protection for victims and address the needs of children exposed to family and domestic violence (Campo, 2015).

One significant shortcoming of the Act is its failure to adequately recognise the diverse challenges faced by Australia's growing multicultural families, particularly those in African Australian communities, when seeking legal protection, accountability, and safety (Laing, 2017). Acknowledging these gaps is essential for ongoing research and publication efforts, such as this book, which aims to inform the law and address the needs of various Australian communities.

Civil Law System Response to Family Violence (FVIOs)

In Australia, each state and territory has introduced legislation addressing family and domestic violence, incorporating a civil remedy known as the intervention order system. This system was regarded as pioneering legislation designed to provide an accessible and free civil option for the protection of victims of violence (Reeves, 2022). It could be accessed by an individual victim or by the police, and, in theory, protection could be obtained 24 hours a day.

However, issues such as inconsistent interpretation, widely varying attitudes among police officers and magistrates, failure to enforce breaches, inadequate training of court staff, a lack of cultural competencies reflecting Australia's diverse communities, language barriers for newly arrived individuals from non-English-speaking backgrounds, and limited access to legal advice and adequate representation—among other challenges—soon led many victims to believe that an intervention order was "not worth the paper it was written on" (Peirce, 2009, p. 48). In short, the legislation itself became a "victim" of prevailing mainstream attitudes, cultural perceptions, and inconsistent enforcement.

Victims can apply for intervention or protection orders, which legally prohibit the perpetrator from contacting or approaching them (Peirce, 2009). These orders aim to enhance the safety of victims and their children. However, one of the principal debates at the time of the system's introduction—and one that continues to this day—is whether legal remedies for family violence should be located within criminal or civil jurisdictions. Questions also persist as to whether this form of legal protection is effectively serving its intended purpose—ensuring victim safety and holding perpetrators accountable—across all Australian communities. Identifying its shortcomings and exploring ways to address them in order to better meet the needs of diverse communities remains an ongoing challenge.

Progress and Impact of FVIOs

Prior to the introduction of protection orders in the 1970s, police responses to family violence were often marked by inaction and a tendency to dismiss women's allegations of abuse (Stanko, 1996). Despite having the authority to treat physical abuse as they would a stranger assault, police frequently advised male perpetrators to "take a walk" when accused of assaulting their spouses (Reeves, 2022).

This approach to intervention differs from African customary practices, where family and community elders intervene through mediation strategies aimed at resolving disputes and maintaining peace within the family, as discussed in the previous chapter. However, the feminist movement prompted a gradual shift towards viewing family violence as a public concern rather than a private matter. The law became the primary tool for addressing this pervasive issue (Reeves, 2022). This focus on criminalisation led to the introduction of new offences, reforms to evidence and sentencing laws, and the establishment of family violence-specific policing policies (Dowling et al., 2018).

While acknowledging that not all family violence incidents are reported, data from police forces across Australia estimates over 700 daily responses to family violence incidents (Blumer, 2016). According to the Australian Bureau of Statistics (ABS) (2024), over 43% of recorded murders—amounting to 97 cases—were related to family and domestic violence. This marks a 10% increase, from 76,900 cases in 2022 to 84,800 in 2023 (ABS, 2024). However, these statistics do not conclusively indicate whether any other forms of intervention and prevention, apart from the issuance of Family Violence Intervention Orders (FVIOs), were implemented prior to the murders. Nevertheless, the data emphasises the widespread prevalence of family violence, underscoring its recognition as a public health concern that requires continuous attention from policymakers, law enforcement, government funding bodies, and empirical research—beyond anecdotal evidence from victim-survivors. In my research, I have observed how these challenges are experienced first-hand by many African Australian applicants and respondents of FVIOs. Cultural misunderstandings, institutional bias, and feelings of alienation frequently mark their interactions with the legal system. This has prompted me to reflect on how these well-intentioned legal interventions can be improved and adapted to meet better the realities and needs of Australia's multicultural communities. It is critical to ensure that legal processes are not only procedurally fair but also culturally responsive, in order to achieve justice and safety for everyone.

Although significant developments have been made in mainstream empirical research to determine whether family violence intervention orders are beneficial or detrimental—particularly in terms of intervention, prevention, and addressing breaches—there remains limited evidence specific to culturally and linguistically diverse (CALD) groups (Douglas & Burdon, 2018; Douglas, 2018a, 2018b). Moreover, a notable research gap exists regarding the impact of FVIOs within migrant and refugee communities, where structural inequalities, discrimination, cultural differences, language barriers, and gender inequality intersect to exacerbate experiences of violence and negative encounters with the Australian legal system (Vaughan et al., 2015, 2016).

Critics of FVIOs, as highlighted by Benitez et al. (2010), Cattaneo et al. (2016), and Cordier et al. (2021), argue that while their usage has increased, evidence of their effectiveness remains mixed due to disparities in their application across countries and states, as well as varying research quality—often biased towards specific communities, approaches, and methodologies.

Studies such as Fraser (2009) on the 'legal problems of African refugees' and Juuk (2023) on African communities—such as 'South Sudanese Australian legal consciousness'—found that cultural practices and beliefs around family dispute resolution and legal matters among African Australian refugee and migrant communities limit their ability to access family law services. This includes seeking legal advice before matters reach crisis point. Furthermore, individuals born in countries where a language other than English is spoken are less likely to recognise family problems as legal issues and, consequently, are less likely to seek legal protection in family matters, such as family violence (Juuk, 2023). Therefore, it is essential to understand the needs of families from African community backgrounds so that processes can be developed to facilitate access to family law services. This would support minority victim-survivors in making informed decisions regarding their safety, ensuring the monitoring of perpetrators, and enhancing the overall safety of their families.

A Uniformed Legal Protection in a Multicultural Society

Despite numerous amendments to the *Family Law Act 1975*, including recent changes recognising same-sex marriage and domestic and family violence in LGBTIQ+ communities, there has been limited focus on the concept of legal pluralism in addressing family violence within Australia. The Australian legal system, despite its white, middle-class Anglo-Celtic origins, now operates within a multicultural society (Juuk, 2023). Laws that successfully encapsulate cultural diversity recognise the multiplicity of "Australian" values—whether derived from cultural, linguistic, racial, religious, or political backgrounds—and seek to protect this diversity against discrimination and intolerance (Fraser, 2009). As interpreters of the law, the courts play a significant role in promoting awareness and respect for other cultures within the wider community.

The debate over the recognition of legal pluralism, particularly customary law, must be understood within the broader function of family law—namely, maintaining the hegemony of Australia's self-perception as a modern, liberal society (Juuk, 2023). Legal pluralism is achievable only if it remains the collective responsibility of society to ensure that resulting legal arrangements are fair and non-discriminatory for all members. Such fairness can protect communities, such as the South Sudanese, from being disadvantaged by the legal system when seeking protection, as discussed in the following chapter on experiences with Family Violence Intervention Orders (FVIOs). Additionally, legal pluralism could help repair the fragile relationship between African Australian communities and the Australian legal system and its practitioners.

Legal pluralism acknowledges that separate personal laws may operate in areas of family law (Berman, 2014; Griffiths, 2011). A personal law system is defined as one in which individuals are subject to the jurisdiction of their own religious-legal norms and institutions concerning matters, such as marriage, maintenance, child custody, and inheritance (Griffiths, 2011). In such systems, an African individual may be subject to customary law, a Jewish person to *Halakhah*, or First Nations people to Indigenous law. Historically, legal pluralism has been a consequence of colonisation. In the fifteenth century, legally pluralistic societies worldwide, particularly in Africa, emerged as a result of European colonisation, as discussed in this chapter. During this period, new laws, rules, and governance systems were introduced, yet Indigenous traditions and customs persisted. Consequently, while colonisers were governed by colonial laws, Indigenous peoples continued to apply their traditional legal systems (Tamanaha, 2021). Colonial and customary laws remained distinct, separated by legal barriers and the limited reach of the colonial legal system, which was largely confined to urban areas (Tamanaha, 2021). The pluralistic nature of legal systems, especially concerning family matters such as family violence, continues to play a crucial role in addressing such issues in Africa, as further explored in Chapter 4.

The debate surrounding the recognition of legal pluralism, particularly customary law, must be understood within the broader context of the function of family law—as an ideology preserving Australia's self-concept as a modern, liberal society (Parashar, 2012). Legal pluralism remains feasible if it is the collective responsibility to ensure resulting legal arrangements are just and non-discriminatory for all members of society. Legal pluralism suggests that distinct personal laws can operate in the realm of family law (Griffiths, 2011). A personal law system is one where individuals are governed by their religious-legal norms and institutions regarding matters such as family violence, marriage, child custody, maintenance, and inheritance (Griffiths, 1986). In such systems, an African might be subject to customary law, and a Jew might adhere to Halakhah. Historically, legal pluralism can be traced back to the consequences of colonisation. In the fifteenth century, European colonisation led to legally pluralistic societies worldwide (Griffiths, 1986). During colonisation, new laws, rules, and governance systems emerged while the traditions and customs of the colonised region persisted. As a result, Indigenous peoples applied their traditional laws, coexisting with colonial laws applicable to the colonisers (Tamanaha, 2008). These legal systems, colonial and customary, were fundamentally distinct, further separated by legal barriers and the limited reach of the legal system, which primarily extended to urban areas (Tamanaha, 2008).

In Australia, there is a single, nationwide legal system, and no official form of legal pluralism exists in personal law areas such as family violence. One attempt to incorporate legal pluralism was made by the Australian Law Reform Commission, which issued a report recommending the recognition of Australian Indigenous law in family law. This led to the establishment of specialised Indigenous legal mechanisms for family violence intervention and prevention (Blagg et al., 2020). However, Aboriginal women remain sceptical of the 'carceral feminism' approach, arguing that family violence is a legacy of colonialism, systemic racism, and intergenerational trauma (Blagg et al., 2020). They advocate for distinct responses separate from the dominant feminist narratives of gender inequality, coercive control, and patriarchy (Blagg et al., 2020). Moreover, the Australian Law Reform Commission's recommendations have lacked adequate implementation of decolonial approaches proposed by Indigenous scholars (Blagg et al., 2020). A subsequent report from Western Australia on the recognition of customary law warned against its implementation, concluding that operating two separate legal systems would be divisive.

The Australian family law approach to family violence is primarily centred on the individual, focusing on victim-survivors—a necessary approach. However, as discussed in Chapter 2, many African individuals face a complex range of experiences related to violence (Shepherd & Spivak, 2020), which contribute to and exacerbate family violence issues. In contrast, customary law approaches to family violence incorporate intervention and prevention strategies that consider victims, perpetrators, and the entire family, rather than focusing solely on individual incidents and perpetrator punishment (Buana & Djanggih, 2018). This broader perspective helps address the needs of all parties involved.

The lack of family violence responses tailored to individual communities' unique needs presents a significant barrier to breaking cycles of abuse within the South Sudanese community. Many existing family services are not culturally responsive and fail to consider the specific challenges faced by African Australians, including racial discrimination, migration trauma, and socioeconomic and intergenerational conflict (Shepherd et al., 2021). These services often adopt a one-size-fits-all approach to perpetrator behaviour change, overlooking structural inequalities, cultural stigmas, and systemic barriers that shape individuals' experiences of violence and accountability (Shepherd et al., 2021). Furthermore, mainstream intervention programs often fail to engage with community leaders, faith-based networks, or culturally specific healing practices, which are crucial for effective change within these communities. Without inclusive and culturally competent services, African Australian families, such as the South Sudanese, may struggle to access meaningful support that fosters accountability while also addressing the root causes of violence—ultimately limiting the effectiveness of family violence prevention efforts.

Conclusion

By examining these aspects, this chapter sheds light on the genesis of the Australian family law system, the reforms that recognise family violence, the introduction of the legal intervention order system, and the need to address diverse social groups. It also identifies gaps where improvements are necessary. Additionally, this chapter highlights how legal pluralism could be better integrated into the Australian legal framework to ensure that all communities, including African Australians such as the South Sudanese community, receive equitable and culturally sensitive legal support, and protection from family violence.

The refusal to recognise certain laws within the Australian family law system, such as those of First Nations people and African Australian customary law, exacerbates the lack of attention to how individuals with colonial histories—such as African Australian former refugees, migrants, and Indigenous communities—engage with both formal and customary legal systems.

The following chapters highlight gaps in the reporting, intervention, and prevention of family violence, police involvement, and legal protection through participants' personal narratives in Chapters 6 and 7. These chapters not only shed light on the experiences of family violence, but also present strategies proposed by the participants for intervention and prevention. These strategies align with the cultural and customary law practices within their communities, as discussed in this chapter, and can work alongside the Australian legal system's approach to family violence, as discussed in this chapter.

References

ABS. (2024). *Recorded crime—Victims-external site opens in new window*. ABS, Australian Government. Accessed 3 March 2025.

Ashkanasy, N. M., Trevor-Roberts, E., & Earnshaw, L. (2002). The Anglo Cluster: Legacy of the British empire. *Journal of World Business, 37*(1), 28–39 [online]. https://doi.org/10.1016/S1090-9516(01)00072-4.

Barwick, G. (1962). The commonwealth marriage act 1961. *Melbourne University Law Review, 3*(3), 277–305.

Barwick, G. (1980). Judiciary law: Some observations thereon. *Current Legal Problems, 33*(1), 239–253. https://doi.org/10.1093/clp/33.1.239

Benitez, C. T., McNiel, D. E., & Binder, R. L. (2010). Do protection orders protect? *The Journal of the American Academy of Psychiatry and the Law, 38*, 376–385.

Berman, P. S. (2014). From legal pluralism to global legal pluralism. *SSRN Electronic Journal*. https://doi.org/10.2139/ssrn.2609369

Blagg, H., Tulich, T., Hovane, V., Raye, D., Worrigal, T., & May, S. (2020). *Understanding the role of Law and Culture in Aboriginal and/or Torres Strait Islander communities in responding to and preventing family violence, Ngarluma/Jaru/Gooniyandi (Hovane), Kimberley and Pilbara region, WA, Jabirr Jabirr/Bardi (Raye), Dampier Peninsula and Kimberley region, WA, Gooniyandi/Gija (Worrigal), Kimberley region, WA (Research report, 19/2020)*. ANROWS.

Blumer, C. (2016). *Australian police deal with domestic violence every two minutes*. ABC News. https://www.abc.net.au/news/2016-04-21/domestic-violence/7341716?nw=0&r=H

Boyle, L. (2015). An Australian august corpus: Why there is only one common law in Australia. *Bond Law Review*. https://doi.org/10.53300/001c.5633

Buana, A. P., & Djanggih, H. (2018). Customary court as alternative to settlement of dispute in South Sulawesi. *Diponegoro Law Review, 3*(2), 154. https://doi.org/10.14710/dilrev.3.2.2018.154-164

Budinski, M., & Gahan, L. (2023). *What is family? Australian views on what makes a family*. Australian Institute of Family Studies.

Campo, M. (2015). *Children's exposure to domestic and family violence: Key issues and responses* (CFCA Paper No. 36). Melbourne: Child Family Community Australia information exchange, Australian Institute of Family Studies.

Cattaneo, L. B., Grossman, J., & Chapman, A. R. (2016). The goals of IPV survivors receiving orders of protection: An application of the empowerment process model. *Journal of Interpersonal Violence, 31*(17), 2889–2911. https://doi.org/10.1177/0886260515581905

Chisholm, R. (2007). Making it work: The Family Law Amendment (Shared Parental Responsibility) Act 2006. *Australian Journal of Family Law, 21*(2), 143–172. https://doi.org/10.3316/agispt.20073884

Cordier, R., Chung, D., Wilkes-Gillan, S., & Speyer, R. (2021). The effectiveness of protection orders in reducing recidivism in domestic violence: A systematic review and meta-analysis. *Trauma, Violence, & Abuse, 22*(4), 804–828. https://doi.org/10.1177/1524838019882361

Cranwell, G. (2001). Treaties and Australian law—Administrative discretions, statutes and the common law. *QUT Law Review, 1*(1). https://doi.org/10.5204/qutlr.v1i1.62

Douglas, H. (2018a). Legal systems abuse and coercive control. *Criminology & Criminal Justice, 18*(1), 84–91. https://doi.org/10.1177/2F1748895817728380

Douglas, H. (2018b). Domestic violence protection orders and their role in ensuring personal security.

Douglas, H., & Burdon, M. (2018). Legal responses to non-consensual smartphone recordings in the context of domestic and family violence. *New South Wales Law Journal, 41*(1), 157–184.

Dowling, C., Morgan, A., Hulme, S., Manning, M., & Wong, G. (2018). Protection orders for domestic violence: A systematic review. *Trends and Issues in Crime and Criminal Justice, 551*, 1–19.

Finlay, H., Bailey-Harris, R. J., & Otlowski, M. (1997). *Family law in Australia* (5th edn). Butterworths (Australia).

Fraser, K. (2009). *Out of Africa and into court: The legal problems of African refugee*. Footscray Community Legal Centre.

Griffiths, J. (1986). What Is Legal Pluralism? *Journal of Legal Pluralism and Unofficial Law, 18*, 1–55. http://dx.doi.org/10.1080/07329113.1986.10756387

Griffiths, A. (2011). Pursuing legal pluralism: The power of paradigms in a global world. *The Journal of Legal Pluralism and Unofficial Law, 43*(64), 173–202. https://doi.org/10.1080/07329113.2011.10756674

Harrison, M. (2005). Review of to have but not to hold: A history of attitudes to marriage and divorce in Australia, 1858–1975 by Henry Finlay (Sydney, The Federation Press, 2005), pp. i–xiv, 1–434. ISBN 1 86287 542 1.

Heley, E., & Hewitt, B. (2022). Same-sex marriage and remarriage in Australia, 2018–2020. *Australian Population Studies, 6*(1), 1–14. https://doi.org/10.37970/aps.v6i1.96.

Hunter, R. (2003). Australian legal histories in context. *Law and History Review, 21*(3), 607–614. https://doi.org/10.2307/3595121

Jacob, H. (1989). Another look at no-fault divorce and the post-divorce finances of women. *Law & Society Review, 23*(1), 95. https://doi.org/10.2307/3053882

Juuk, B. G. A. (2023). *Family dispute resolution from a cultural perspective.* Cambridge Scholars Publishing.

Laing, L. (2017). Secondary victimization: Domestic violence survivors navigating the family law system. *Violence against Women, 23*(11), 1314–1335. https://doi.org/10.1177/1077801216659942

Parashar, A. (2012). Australian Muslims and Family Law: Diversity and Gender Justice. *Journal of Intercultural Studies, 33*(5), 565–583. https://doi.org/10.1080/07256868.2012.701611

Peirce, J. (2009). Family Violence Protection Act 2008. *Family Matters, 83,* 48–51.

Rabe, M., & Kumswa, S. (2022). Families in Africa: Economic hardships and intergenerational support: Special issue: South African Review of Sociology (SARS). *South African Review of Sociology, 52*(4), 1–4. https://doi.org/10.1080/21528586.2023.2180428

Reeves, E. (2022). The potential introduction of police-issued family violence intervention orders in Victoria, Australia: Considering the unintended consequences. *Current Issues in Criminal Justice, 34*(2), 207–218. https://doi.org/10.1080/10345329.2021.2021721

Shepherd, S. M., & Spivak, B. L. (2020). Estimating the extent and nature of offending by Sudanese-born individuals in Victoria. *Australian and New Zealand Journal of Criminology, 53*(3), 352–368. https://doi.org/10.1177/0004865820929066

Shepherd, S., Bailey, A., & Masuka, G. (2021). The experiences and perspectives of African-Australian community service providers who work with at-risk and justice-involved youth. *International Journal of Offender Therapy and Comparative Criminology, 66*(13–14), 1432–1453. https://doi.org/10.1177/0306624X211022652 (Original work published 2022).

Stanko, E. A. (1996). Warnings to women: Police advice and women's safety in Britain. *Violence against Women, 2*(1), 5–24. https://doi.org/10.1177/1077801296002001002

Tamanaha, B. Z. (2008). Understanding legal pluralism: past to present, local to global. *The Sydney Law Review, 30*(3), 375–411. https://search.informit.org/doi/10.3316/agispt.20084529

Tamanaha, B.Z. (2021). Legal pluralism across the global South: Colonial origins and contemporary consequences. *The Journal of Legal Pluralism and Unofficial Law*, 1–38. https://doi.org/10.1080/07329113.2021.1942606.

Vaughan, C., Davis, E., Murdolo, A., Chen, J., Murray, L., Quiazon, R., Block, K., & Warr, D. (2016). *Promoting community-led responses to violence against immigrant and refugee women in metropolitan and regional Australia.* The ASPIRE Project: Research report (ANROWS Horizons 07/2016). Sydney: Australia's National Research Organisation for Women's Safety.

Vaughan, C., Murdolo, A., Murray, L., Davis, E., Chen, J., Block, K., Quiazon, R., & Warr, D. (2015). ASPIRE: A multi-site community-based participatory research project to increase understanding of the dynamics of violence against immigrant and refugee women in Australia. *BMC Public Health, 15*, 1283. https://doi.org/10.1186/s12889-015-2634-0

Williams, G. (2005). The Australian constitution: A documentary history (Melbourne University Press, Carlton 2005). *Oxford University Commonwealth Law Journal, 5*(2), 317–321. https://doi.org/10.1080/14729342.2005.11421462

6

Victims Experiences of Family Violence Intervention: Fear of Australian Police and Legal System

Introduction

In the previous chapter, I discussed the establishment of Australian family law, its amendments—including those aimed at protecting women and children—and its role in divorce proceedings and addressing family violence. I also examined the introduction of family violence legislation and protection orders across Australian states and territories, highlighting their significance in safeguarding victims. Additionally, I explored the disparities between African customary law approaches to family violence and the Australian legal framework, the absence of legal pluralism in Australia, and how these factors challenge the notion of a truly multicultural society. Specifically, I examined how African communities such as the South Sudanese are inadequately addressed through the one-size-fits-all approach of the Australian legal system.

Intervention and prevention of family violence in Australia require the collaboration of multiple stakeholders, including the legal system (Campbell et al., 2023; Lloyd et al., 2023). For instance, law enforcement agencies, particularly the police, often serve as the first point of contact in cases of family violence. Their role is critical in responding to incidents, issuing interim safety orders where necessary, ensuring the

A. K. Anyieth, *Decolonising Family Violence Legal Intervention Orders in African-Australian Communities*, https://doi.org/10.1007/978-3-031-95404-7_6

victim's protection, and either removing or arresting the perpetrator if warranted (e.g. in cases of assault) (Campbell et al., 2021). However, for police action to be taken, incidents must be reported—whether by victims, neighbours, bystanders, or service providers. Unfortunately, within the South Sudanese community, many cases of family violence go unreported or are only reported at crisis points, as confirmed by the participants' narratives in this chapter.

This chapter will highlight the difficult decisions victims must make when experiencing family violence and the factors influencing their interactions with state institutions, particularly the police. The chapter considers elements such as community norms, societal stigmas, and the availability—or absence—of support systems. Fieldwork data reveals that, in many cases, victims do not perceive police involvement as a viable or desirable option. These findings challenge mainstream narratives in the family violence sector, which often assume that seeking help necessarily involves legal intervention through the police. This chapter will explore how these perspectives contradict prevailing assumptions about legal remedies and expose broader flaws within the Australian policing system, including its colonial roots, its relationship with the South Sudanese community, and possible approaches to decolonising its embedded colonial structures.

Colonial Policing

The policing of family violence in Australia has been criticised for perpetuating the historical and ongoing effects of colonialism, particularly in Indigenous communities (Blagg & Anthony, 2019; Hovane, 2015) and culturally and linguistically diverse (CALD) communities, such as African Australians. The standardised policing model in Australia has often marginalised the voices and specific needs of these communities, creating a complex and, at times, distrustful relationship with law enforcement.

Historically, police forces in settler societies were established to maintain order, often reinforcing colonial control rather than protecting marginalised communities (Blagg & Anthony, 2019). Many communities affected by settler colonialism continue to view law enforcement as an instrument of state power rather than a safeguard for community safety (Blagg & Anthony, 2019; Hovane, 2015). Consequently, the policing of family violence has often been inadequate or culturally insensitive, leading to frequent criticism.

As discussed in Chapter 3, the experiences of family violence within the South Sudanese community are shaped by factors such as acculturation, trauma, socioeconomic disadvantage, the impacts of colonisation, and shifting gender roles. However, policing practices have been criticised for failing to acknowledge these complexities. Instead, responses have sometimes prioritised punitive measures over culturally sensitive interventions. Blagg et al. (2022) argue that colonial legacies—such as historical violence, socioeconomic marginalisation, and intergenerational trauma—must be recognised in addressing family violence in settler-colonial communities. As Aboriginal women have highlighted, family violence must be understood within a historical framework shaped by colonialism, systemic disadvantage, cultural dislocation, the forced removal of children, and intergenerational trauma (Blagg et al., 2022, p. 536).

The fragile relationship between policing and marginalised communities exacerbates experiences of family violence and hinders the development of adequate intervention and prevention strategies. Addressing family violence effectively requires a broader approach that acknowledges the social, cultural, and economic inequalities created by colonisation—inequalities that continue to serve as root causes of violence within these communities.

Policing African Communities

The historical context surrounding the interactions between police and African Australian communities is deeply rooted in systemic issues that reflect broader societal inequities. African Australian experience of 'othering' has perpetuated a policing model often characterised by mistrust and a lack of cultural sensitivity (Ali et al., 2023; Gwakuba,

2022). This disconnection is exacerbated by institutionalised racism, wherein policing practices disproportionately target minority groups, leading to heightened tensions and negative encounters (Ali et al., 2023; Gwakuba, 2022). Historical injustices, such as forced regulations and the suppression of cultural identity, continue to influence the dynamics between these communities and law enforcement, creating grounds for conflict (Sharp & Atherton, 2007). African communities' mistrust of law enforcement is especially harmful in cases of family violence, where early intervention and protection are critical. When victims do not feel safe or supported by the police, they are less likely to report abuse, cooperate with legal processes, or access the justice and support systems available to them. This tainted relationship undermines not only individual safety but also broader public trust in institutions designed to protect, perpetuating cycles of silence and vulnerability in already marginalised communities.

Research indicates that public perceptions of migrants and refugees, particularly men—including many African Australians—are frequently linked to crime, perpetuating harmful stereotypes that influence police encounters (Ali et al., 2023; Hopkins & Popovic, 2024). These stereotypes sometimes result in over-policing, inappropriate family violence interventions, and increased scrutiny of these communities, leading to a cycle of negativity that further entrenches feelings of alienation and hostility (Hopkins & Popovic, 2024). Additionally, Australia's evolving ethnic diversity highlights the necessity for local governments and police to foster intercultural understanding. Improved community relations depend on recognising historical injustices and implementing proactive engagement initiatives.

Police involvement in incidents of family violence in Australia plays a pivotal role in intervention and prevention. As the initial point of contact, the police response can significantly influence victim safety, perpetrator accountability, punitive measures, and the overall outcomes for all parties involved, including affected family members (Meyer, 2010; Barlow & Walklate, 2018; Douglas, 2019; Reeves, 2021). In every state and territory in Australia, the police are required to take action if they deem a person to be in danger of family violence. Thus, if police intervention occurs only when the violence has reached a critical point, the necessary actions may be drastic—such as removing individuals from the premises and involving child protection services. If police were engaged at an earlier stage, they might be able to de-escalate the situation and provide referral information for those experiencing family violence. However, for many participants whose narratives are analysed and discussed in this chapter, there was a marked reluctance to involve law enforcement, often meaning that police were only called when the violence had escalated to a critical juncture.

This reluctance can be attributed to African Australians' ongoing negative experiences with the legal system, which shape their legal consciousness (as briefly discussed in Chapter 2), their perception of themselves before the law, and their views on Australian police and law. Additionally, this reluctance is influenced by the general community's negative experiences with the police and their interactions with individuals of African Australian backgrounds, as highlighted by participants:

Lisa, female participant:	In our community, people don't usually involve the police in many situations where others might. The police in this country haven't been very supportive of us, so individuals call them only when they have nowhere else to turn or are facing physical assault.
Mabior, male participant:	The police have not been helpful towards our community since we arrived here. You've seen the news, especially here in Melbourne, Victoria—they paint us all as criminals. The whole 'African Gang' issue affects us in so many ways.
Akuol, female participant:	I didn't want to call the police because the police have not been nice to our community.

The above statements highlight the existing negative relationship between the community and the police, which influences victims of family violence to avoid involving law enforcement unless absolutely necessary. The decision to stay in abusive relationships and distrust law enforcement is shaped by community experiences, fostering negative perceptions of authorities.

Participants also described hostile police behaviour towards many African Australians, particularly young men, which is often sensationalised by various news outlets in Australia. Some, like Charl, recounted instances of excessive force during arrests and detentions without proper investigation:

Charl, male participant: When they were arresting me, they threw me to the ground, and I hit my head on the concrete, even though I wasn't resisting or fighting them. They took me to the station and kept me there for a very long time.

Achol, female participant: We reconciled within 6 months because of extended family intervention not because the police arrested him. Police did nothing other than to give us a paper [FVIO document]. There was no further support after that, so I never try to involve them again.

A key consequence of this experience-based fear of the police across African communities, according to participants, is their reluctance to seek police assistance in cases of family violence. As a result, police involvement often occurs only when the violence has reached a critical stage, leading to arrests involving excessive force and the implementation of significant institutional measures, including but not limited to Family Violence Intervention Orders (FVIOs) and the involvement of child protection services.

Adau, female participant: In our community, we fear the police because many of them have been hostile towards us Africans here in Australia. Especially when you have this skin tone [meaning black skin], they see you as different.

Nyamar, female participant: When we had a conflict, my in-laws mediated because they said there was no need to involve the police. The police would just remove the man [her husband] but never solve the issue.

Mary, female participant: Until the change their negative views about our community, victims will always struggle to involve the police.

As a result of this well-founded fear and distrust of the police, many victims advocate for more culturally sensitive and effective support mechanisms alongside police involvement and legal interventions such as FVIOs.

Akuol, female participant: Reporting family violence can be very challenging for young South Sudanese individuals. I never wanted to report until the violence was really bad. It got physical and I was scared for my life. The relationship between us and the police is not good. As a result, even when I was experiencing family violence, I felt very reluctant to engage with law enforcement.

The negative experiences that South Sudanese young people have had with the police often lead them to hesitate in seeking help when they become victims of family violence, as Akuol highlighted. Whether they are direct victims or witnesses of such violence, they may fear that involving the police will exacerbate their situation rather than provide the protection they need. Concerns about being dismissed, not taken seriously, or even criminalised themselves often prevent many from reporting abuse. Some young people also worry that police intervention could result in family separation or increased community stigma. As a result, without trust in the legal system, young South Sudanese women who experience family violence may suffer in silence, remain trapped in unsafe environments, or turn to informal solutions that fall short of offering adequate protection. Addressing this issue requires culturally sensitive policing, active community engagement, and efforts to rebuild trust between South Sudanese youth and law enforcement.

Decolonising Family Violence Policing

The role of law enforcement, particularly the police, is crucial in addressing incidents of family violence. Police often act as the primary responders and gatekeepers of the criminal justice system, ensuring victim protection, enforcing the law, maintaining peace, and facilitating access to support and treatment services (Mazerolle et al., 2018). However, over the years, police have frequently been criticised for their unsupportive and unsympathetic responses to intimate partner violence (IPV) cases (Goodman-Delahunty & Crehan, 2015; Meyer et al., 2021).

While police stations have established family violence units—a positive step (Islam et al., 2024)—the experiences of participants in this research suggest that these reforms have not significantly improved the relationship between African communities, such as the South Sudanese, and the police. As a result, there is a need to decolonise the policing of family violence and reform the Family Violence Intervention Order (FVIO) system by addressing colonial-era law enforcement practices that often prioritise punitive responses over community-centred, survivor-led approaches.

In many post-colonial states, contemporary policing remains shaped by its colonial past. Colonial police forces were designed to serve imperial authorities rather than local populations, and this legacy persists in the form of militarised policing, corruption, and human rights abuses (Blagg et al., 2022). Many law enforcement agencies in settler-colonial countries such as Australia continue to operate with excessive force, a lack of accountability, and deep mistrust from the communities they serve. Decolonising policing in these regions involves shifting law enforcement away from its colonial-era function of repression towards community-oriented and rights-based policing. This requires structural reforms, increased local governance, and investment in non-coercive approaches to justice, such as restorative and community-based models.

To decolonise policing in cases of family violence, law enforcement must shift from a top-down, punitive approach to one that centres on the needs, voices, and cultural contexts of survivors. This involves integrating restorative justice practices, community-led interventions, and culturally informed support services that empower survivors and rehabilitate perpetrators (further discussed in Chapter 9), rather than reinforcing systemic inequalities through criminalisation.

Additionally, decolonising family violence policing requires addressing the historical mistrust between marginalised communities and law enforcement by ensuring greater accountability, representation, and collaboration with grassroots organisations. By prioritising survivor safety, perpetrator rehabilitation, social and racial equality, community healing, and culturally responsive solutions, policing can move away from colonial frameworks and become a trusted tool for justice rather than a mechanism of oppression.

Conclusion

This chapter explores victims' experiences with the state justice system, focusing on the complex decisions they face when navigating family violence. It examines the factors shaping their interactions with institutions such as the police, including community norms, societal stigma, and the availability of support systems. Fieldwork data reveals that many victims do not always view police intervention as a viable or desirable option, challenging mainstream narratives that equate seeking help with legal action. By highlighting these perspectives, the chapter sheds light on broader systemic issues within the Australian policing system.

The chapter outlines the colonial context of Australian policing and the enduring colonial structures that remain in place. It argues that, due to this complex history, victims of family violence from the South Sudanese community—often distrust the police and hesitate to seek their intervention. This reluctance stems from negative past experiences with law enforcement, which contribute to a broader distrust of the legal system within many African Australian communities. For example, as discussed in Chapter 2, African Australians are overrepresented in the criminal justice system, further reinforcing these concerns.

By highlighting these challenges, this chapter provides a more nuanced understanding of why many victims of family violence from the South Sudanese community are hesitant to engage with the state, particularly the police, as a source of safety and protection. It also acknowledges the difficulties law enforcement faces when addressing family violence issues. Consequently, the chapter concludes with a call for the decolonisation of police systems and structures that disadvantage marginalised communities, such as the South Sudanese community.

In the following chapter, I discussed the empirical findings related to experiences of FVIO applicants and respondents from the South Sudanese community.

References

Ali, M. M., Shepherd, S., & Ahmed (Shiday), B. M. (2023). Promoting trust and police legitimacy in African Australian communities: A critical reflection on community engagement strategies and practical recommendations for police. *International Journal of Police Science & Management, 25*(1), 146135572211455. https://doi.org/10.1177/14613557221145593

Barlow, C., & Walklate., S. (2018, January 19). Policing intimate partner violence: The 'golden thread' of discretion. *Policing: A Journal of Policy and Practice*. Epub ahead of print. https://doi.org/10.1093/police/pay001.

Blagg, H., & Anthony, T. (2019). *Decolonising criminology: Imagining justice in a postcolonial world*. Palgrave Macmillan UK.

Blagg, H., Hovane, V., Tulich, T., Raye, D., May, S., & Worrigal, T. (2022). Law, culture and decolonisation: The perspectives of aboriginal elders on family violence in Australia. *Social & Legal Studies, 31*(4), 535–558. https://doi.org/10.1177/09646639211046134

Campbell, E., Bissett, T., Howard, A., Lewers, N., Polis, M., & Richter, J. (2021). *More than just a piece of paper: Getting protection orders made in a safe and supported way: Responding to recommendation 77 of the royal commission into family violence* (pp. 1–130). Centre for Innovative Justice, RMIT University.

Campbell, E., Ellard, R., Hew, E., Simpson, M., McCann, B., & Meyer, S. (2023). *WRAP around families experiencing AVITH: Towards a collaborative service response* (Research report, 04/2023). ANROWS.

Douglas, H. (2019). Policing domestic and family violence. *International Journal for Crime, Justice and Social Democracy, 8*(2), 31–49. https://doi.org/10.5204/ijcjsd.v8i2.1122

Goodman-Delahunty, J., & Crehan, A. C. (2015). Enhancing police responses to domestic violence incidents. *Violence against Women, 22*(8), 1007–1026. https://doi.org/10.1177/1077801215613854

Gwakuba, U. (2022). *Police engagement with African communities in Western Australia.* Edith Cowan University. https://ro.ecu.edu.au/theses/2565

Hopkins, T., & Popovic, G. (2024). Do Australian police engage in racial profiling? A method for identifying racial profiling in the absence of police data. *Current Issues in Criminal Justice, 37*(1), 19–40. https://doi.org/10.1080/10345329.2024.2326709

Hovane, V. (2015). Our story to tell: Aboriginal perspectives on domestic and family violence. *ANROWS Footprints, 1*, 13–17.

Islam, M. J., Suzuki, M., & Mazerolle, P. (2024). Police responses to intimate partner violence incidents involving children: Exploring variations in actions and concerns in an Australian jurisdiction. *Child Abuse & Neglect, 147*, 1–13. https://doi.org/10.1016/j.chiabu.2023.106568

Lloyd, J., Dembele, L., Dawes, C., Jane, S., & Macmillan, L. (2023). *The Australian National Research Agenda to end violence against women and children (ANRA) 2023–2028.* ANROWS.

Mazerolle, L., Eggins, E., Sydes, M., Hine, L., McEwan, J., Norrie, G., & Somerville, A. (2018). Criminal justice responses to domestic and family violence: A rapid review of the evaluation literature.

Meyer, S. (2010). Seeking help to protect the children? The influence of children on women's decisions to seek help when experiencing intimate partner violence. *Journal of Family Violence, 25*(8), 713–725. https://doi.org/10.1007/s10896-010-9329-1

Meyer, S., Reeves, E., & Fitz-Gibbon, K. (2021). The intergenerational transmission of family violence: Mothers' perceptions of children's experiences and use of violence in the home. *Child & Family Social Work, 26*(3), 476–484. https://doi.org/10.1111/cfs.12830

Reeves, E. (2021). 'I'm not at all protected and I think other women should know that, that they're not protected either': Victim–survivors' experiences of 'misidentification' in Victoria's family violence system. *International*

Journal for Crime, Justice and Social Democracy, 10(4), 39–51. https://doi.org/10.5204/ijcjsd.1992

Sharp, D., & Atherton, S. (2007). To serve and protect? The experiences of policing in the community of young people from black and other ethnic minority groups. *The British Journal of Criminology, 47*(5), 746–763. http://www.jstor.org/stable/23639304

Wheelock, D., Stroshine, M. S., & O'Hear, M. (2018). Disentangling the relationship between race and attitudes toward the police: Police contact, perceptions of safety, and procedural justice. *Crime & Delinquency, 65*(7), 001112871881192. https://doi.org/10.1177/0011128718811928

7

Applicants and Respondents Experiences of Family Violence Intervention Orders

Introduction

In the previous chapter, I explored what happens when a family violence incident occurs, including the role of the police and African Australian views on law enforcement, particularly the police as a tool for protection. I also discussed the coloniality of policing in Australia and some of the reasons participants preferred not to involve the police. To continue analysing experiences of family violence and intervention orders, this chapter delves into the experiences of South Sudanese applicants and respondents of Family Violence Intervention Orders (FVIOs) following instances of family violence. Within this chapter, I present participants' narratives concerning the legal responses they encountered in relation to their experiences of family violence. This includes legal interventions through the police and court systems, as well as the procedural aspects of the family violence intervention order system.

The chapter explores the implementation of FVIOs, assessing their effectiveness and the consequences faced by both applicants and respondents as a result of these orders. In addition, it presents participants' accounts of the broader implications and challenges they have encountered due to FVIOs. These implications encompass the involvement of

A. K. Anyieth, *Decolonising Family Violence Legal Intervention Orders in African-Australian Communities*, https://doi.org/10.1007/978-3-031-95404-7_7

services such as child protection, which can disrupt family units and result in feelings of shame and stigma.

The chapter also considers the impact on affected family members (AFMs), referring to individuals within the African family dynamic, including children, siblings from both sides, parents, aunties, and uncles. Furthermore, it examines the broader community's involvement and response when family violence occurs.

Family Violence Intervention Orders (FVIOs)

Previous research has shown that respondents and applicants from Culturally and Linguistically Diverse (CALD) backgrounds often report a limited understanding of the FVIO process, and the specific conditions outlined in the orders, beyond the mere removal of the FVIO respondent (Campbell et al., 2021). They only understand the conditions when a legal representative takes sufficient time to explain the orders (Campbell et al., 2021). Aligning with these previous studies, my findings in this chapter provide specific details about the experiences of South Sudanese navigating FVIOs. They demonstrate that not only does the incomprehensibility of the FVIO process leads to potential breaches, but it can also result in escalations in violence and a further loss of agency or sense of control for both applicants and affected family members. This chapter seeks to highlight the gaps and areas for improvement in both cultural and legal responses to family violence, ultimately transitioning into the following chapter, which discusses participants' preference for effective and culturally sensitive approaches to intervention and support.

I now turn to one of the main research questions that this research addresses: whether Family Violence Intervention Orders (FVIOs) effectively achieve their intended purpose of halting violence and abusive behaviours within the South Sudanese Australian community. The findings in this part of the book are particularly important as they reveal new knowledge about the impact of FVIOs as tools for protection in the South Sudanese community.

However, before reporting participants' experiences, I briefly outline the relevant application processes. The FVIO process is unclear, and participants have experienced the earliest stages as confusing and distressing. My findings reveal that the intervention process is confusing, aligning with previous research concerning the mainstream population. However, for my participants, this confusion is intensified due to the effects of acculturation—many being former refugees—language barriers, and cultural nuances that intersect with Australian legal approaches. For many, this confusion led to potential breaches of orders and escalations in violence. Of particular note is one participant's description of the process as victimising (demonstrated in the quotes below). This speaks to participants' accounts of intervention orders being actioned without their control or agency.

In most states and territories in Australia, there are several ways to apply for an FVIO, including (1) calling triple zero to receive a Family Violence Safety Notice (FVSN) issued by the police, (2) submitting a paper-based application at the nearest police station, or (3) submitting an online application. FVIOs can also be initiated by third parties, such as the police or community service providers working with the family and/or victims. However, it is important to note that at the time when this research data was collected, there was a lack of coherence and consistency in this process.

John-S recounted his experience of confusion when he was issued an FVIO without proper explanation. His account echoes those of other participants, who felt unsure about what the FVIOs meant in practical terms and frustrated in their attempts to seek help in understanding how to avoid breaching these orders:

> *John-S, male participant:* The police officer who handed me the paper was very impolite. She said, "You shouldn't call her. You shouldn't message her on Facebook." I looked at the paper and asked, "What is this?" She, a female police officer, replied, "There are several things here. Take this one: You shouldn't contact her," referring to my wife. Due to the presence of people around, she couldn't read the details to me, I assumed. I further inquired, "What is this?" She responded, "You should read it. You shouldn't contact her, and you have to be in court on such and such date." That's what she told me. This is my first time ever being in court and my first accusation, including family violence.

The lack of clarity regarding the FVIO and its specific conditions left John and other participants, whose experiences will be discussed below, feeling vulnerable to breaching it. In our conversation, John mentioned that he had complied with all the conditions of the FVSN and later the FVIO. However, he expressed a desire for someone to have explained the paperwork to him before he left the police station. He wanted a clear understanding of all the conditions and who was included in the order. He was uncertain whether his teenage boys, who lived with him, were included in the order, given that they had also been residing in the same house as the applicant before she moved out.

In addition, such confusion and lack of understanding of FVIOs are compounded by language barriers for some participants, such as Atem, who come from a refugee background with limited access to education before migrating to Australia. Atem's account highlights the significance of language barriers in exacerbating the incomprehensibility of FVIOs:

> *Atem, male participant:* My biggest challenge, among other things, was language and understanding. I didn't understand things [conditions of the order] properly. I felt my rights were being taken from me, and there was nothing I could do about it simply because I couldn't speak proper English.
>
> *Ajokdit, male participant:* The court proceedings move very quickly, and both you and the interpreter are expected to keep pace and fully comprehend everything that is happening. At times, the court officials do not realise how challenging it can be for non-English speakers to follow and understand the proceedings. Until this issue is addressed, members of our community will continue to leave the court feeling confused and frustrated.

The lack of comprehensibility or support in helping respondents understand the orders and how to comply with them appeared to lead to accidental breaches, defiance due to a lack of comprehension and respect for the orders, and, in some cases, escalations in violence. Comprehension here goes beyond simply having an interpreter translate the order from English into the respondent's native language; it also includes assessing the respondent's cognitive understanding of the order's conditions. These issues were particularly evident in the accounts of female participants:

> *Tina, female participant:* They don't understand them. They don't respect them. Most times, I've seen violence continue even after an order is issued—sometimes it becomes even more violent than before. I have experienced and witnessed this so often in our community.
> *Sarah, female participant:* They themselves don't comprehend this document [intervention order] or its seriousness most of the time. So, what they tend to do is either move far away from the victim and then provoke them by letting the whole community know that they've been 'kicked out' of the house by their wife, or they move out and become even angrier and more violent.

In their interviews, Sarah and Tina reflect on men in their communities who have received FVIOs. Both women observe that the respondents often do not understand the conditions of FVIOs, which leads to a lack of respect for and adherence to the orders. Additionally, both women link this misunderstanding to an increase in violence, highlighting a significant issue: the incomprehensibility of FVIOs contributes to their ineffectiveness and, in some cases, exacerbates the very violence they are meant to prevent.

This issue is further compounded by the experience of being victimised by the FVIO process, as described by both respondents and affected family members in this research. Many participants expressed that they did not fully understand what was happening, particularly when the process was conducted by external parties. This lack of agency is evident in the experiences of Tina and Deng:

> *Tina, female participant:* Our doctor reported the violence, I think. He was threatening to kill me, and the police came. I believe the doctor had already reported it before he got home from his appointment. He was arrested, and I was given the paperwork that separated us. The whole process was handled by other people, the doctor and the police, it was so fast and very confusing. I didn't understand who was doing or saying what.

In Tina's account, the rapid enforcement of the FVIO added to her confusion. The process, which led to a sudden and dramatic separation from her husband, was initiated and carried out by others, leaving her feeling powerless and unaware of what was happening. Despite the profound impact of the FVIO on her life, including the breakup of her family, she felt she had no control over the situation.

Deng's experience mirrors Tina's in terms of confusion, the rapid escalation of events, and a sense of powerlessness:

> *Deng, male participant:* It was my first time interacting with the police. I had no idea what was happening. Everything happened so fast, and they didn't want to listen to both sides before escalating the case to court. There were a lot of things that should have been done before imposing the FVIO conditions. But if you try to explain this to the police, they say, 'You are challenging their law.' But their law and processes are confusing and victimise us in some ways.

As Deng highlights, the complexities of obtaining an FVIO can feel victimising for both respondents and affected family members. The FVIO process is objectively unclear, and this confusion is exacerbated for participants due to language barriers and the rapid processing of orders. However, this confusion is not merely procedural—it contributes to a more distressing experience in which participants feel victimised by a system that operates beyond their control.

Misunderstanding or misinterpreting the order conditions, particularly by respondents, poses a significant risk of breach and further erodes trust in the legal system as an effective means of family violence intervention within their communities. Participants such as Tina and Sarah expressed that when respondents do not understand the orders due to ignorance, language barriers, and a lack of culturally sensitive support, they are set up for failure. Applicants and those affected by violence are also at risk of further victimisation—whether the breach is intentional or not.

Participants widely expressed concerns that without clear explanations, consistent monitoring, culturally safe follow-ups, and additional support resources, FVIOs provide only temporary safety before situations revert to previous patterns of violence. This concern was widespread, with every participant raising the issue unprompted, though they articulated it in different ways. This underscores the severity of these barriers and the confusion they create, ultimately to the detriment of both respondents and affected family members.

As demonstrated in the cases of John-S and Atem, the effectiveness of FVIOs was undermined when law enforcement officers failed to explain the order, its conditions, and the consequences of breaching it. This lack of clarity often led to escalations in violence, worsening the situation after the removal of the violent partner from the family. Regardless of how participants expressed their concerns, the core message remains the same: without clarity before issuing FVIOs, during the monitoring phase, and in post-intervention support, these orders have minimal impact in achieving their intended purpose of halting violence.

Rushed Court Process and Lack of Appropriate Legal Representation

Continuing from the lack of clarity regarding Family Violence Intervention Orders (FVIOs) and the confusion experienced by both applicants and respondents, many participants—particularly respondents—reported receiving insufficient legal support before and during FVIO court proceedings. Although services such as those provided by Legal Aids (VLA) offer legal advice to respondents in court, participants encountered difficulties in accessing this support.

There is no doubt that Australian courts are often overwhelmed by the number of cases that must appear before a magistrate in a single day. Participants explained that when a lawyer was appointed, the process felt rushed, and respondents felt that their side of the story was not adequately heard, as described by Atem below. Respondents who had sought legal advice from duty lawyers stated that the hurried nature of the process, caused by high demand, intensified their sense of neglect. In numerous cases, they felt pressured by lawyers to consent to the order and its conditions rather than contest it, simply to expedite proceedings.

This lack of legal support can have detrimental effects on respondents' understanding of the FVIO and their ability to comply with its terms, further endangering victims and at-risk family members, as highlighted by Lisa:

> *Atem, male participant*: The most painful part was that even when I tried to speak, they didn't want to listen. How can you represent someone if you don't even know what happened? It felt like they just wanted to hand me the paper [intervention order]—end of the story.
> *Lisa, female participant:* I was happy to be protected, but I also think that he didn't understand the depth of what that paper meant, and he didn't receive any help during or after the FVIO. They just asked him not to contact me or the kids. I don't think that helped him or me at all.

Both Atem and Lisa's experiences highlight significant limitations in the FVIO process. Their accounts demonstrate that when due process is neglected, both applicants and respondents are at risk of not fully complying with the order's conditions. If respondents lack a clear understanding of the process and the order itself, there is a risk that victim protection could be short-lived.

Concerns were also raised by both respondents and applicants about the lack of clarity regarding the roles of individuals in court. Participants' accounts indicate confusion about the distinction between legal information and legal advice provided by their representatives. For example, explaining a family violence services brochure to an applicant would not be considered legal advice. However, a legal practitioner advising an applicant or respondent on the consequences of breaching the order and the appropriate steps to take would constitute legal advice. The period between respondents being served and when they receive legal advice—or have a family member help explain the conditions—may leave room for both unintended and intended breaches.

Many participants were uncertain about the roles of the individuals they encountered during the process, often unsure whether they were speaking to a lawyer, a family violence service provider, or a social worker. Some only discovered later that the person they had spoken with was a family violence court liaison officer, not a lawyer, as Deng recounted:

> *Deng, male participant:* One woman came into the room, and we talked for a bit—I thought she was my lawyer. Then later, someone else came in and said she was my lawyer (apparently, the first person was from court services), and I was wondering what was going on. How many lawyers do I have to speak to?
>
> *Mabior, male participant:* The first time we went to court, they all sat with my wife and asked me to sit somewhere else. I sat by myself. Neither of us knew what was going on or how long we were supposed to be there. It was a confusing process for both of us.
>
> *Achan, female participant:* His English is not good, so I was worried that he wouldn't even understand the document [intervention order document] that was given to him. Our uncle, who went with him, said he [her husband] didn't receive much help when they went to court, and now he is even angrier.

A significant common thread in these stories is that many South Sudanese individuals affected by FVIOs have found the experience deeply confusing. They report a lack of support, uncertainty around legal representation, and a poor understanding of what an FVIO entails and how to comply with one. The implications of this lack of understanding and support are serious, with participants reporting increased anger, further violence within families, and criminal consequences due to unintended breaches. These experiences highlight the urgent need for a decolonial approach to family violence intervention and prevention within African Australian communities.

Cultural Dynamics and Practices that Collide with Enforcement of FVIOs

The primary intention of FVIOs is to ensure the safety of the applicant by removing the respondent from the same physical space or by maintaining a certain distance between them (Australian Human Rights Commission [AHRC], 2010). However, in the context of many African families, the traditional Western definition of a family—consisting of two parents and a few children—may not be applicable (Deng, 2016a, 2016b). South Sudanese families are often large, with extended family members considered part of the household, and they may all live in close proximity (Elmusharaf et al., 2017). The Western cultural paradigm, among other factors, influences the notion of personal safety (AHRC, 2010), as Western societies tend to be more individualistic than non-Western cultures. In a collectivist cultural context such as African communities, proximity is often crucial for well-being, whereas from a Western legal perspective, physical closeness can sometimes pose a risk to victims' safety. This dynamic makes the enforcement of FVIOs more complex in these communities compared to mainstream Australian society, as Garang explains below.

> *Garang, male participant:* We attended the same church. We are from the same clan, which means that at every community occasion I am invited to, she will most likely be invited as well because our relatives have a good relationship. Sometimes, they invite us both without knowing that the other party has also been invited. So, these things made it hard to stay far from each other as the court ordered.

Garang's narrative highlights that communal beliefs and practices are not considered when enforcing FVIOs in the South Sudanese community, which hampers the order's success in achieving its intended purpose. In many African cultures, marriage is regarded as a cornerstone of society. It is a fundamental social and cultural institution that strengthens community bonds and ensures the continuation of family lineages through procreation and child-rearing (Baloyi, 2022; Mafela, 2016; Ndlovu & Naidoo, 2023). Consequently, the approval of parents, siblings, and extended family members is essential for a couple's union (Deng, 2016a, 2016b). Due to this communal involvement in intimate relationships, ending a relationship, especially through a legal intervention rather than within the family or community becomes challenging for those involved. Extended families and the community struggle to accept these new legal restrictions, which essentially force them to choose which member of the couple to invite to family or community events (Deng, 2016; O'Byrne, 2021).

> *Achol, female participant:* I called the police, and we went to court, where he was given a 200-metre restraining order for my safety, his safety, and the safety of the children. We couldn't see each other, but that became very difficult because he was well-known in the community—he was not a bad person; I was just angry. It was challenging because now our relatives and the community had to choose between us when there was a family or community occasion. At first, we tried to keep the intervention order hidden, but it became difficult not to attend family events, especially those nearby.

Individuals like Achol, who deal with family violence within the South Sudanese while navigating multiple social and legal challenges, often unintentionally breach FVIOs. For instance, in families that live in close proximity or regularly visit each other to foster social cohesion, FVIO breaches may occur if a respondent visits another family member while the protected person is also present. Additionally, cultural dynamics related to communal places of worship, such as churches and mosques (as mentioned above by Garang), can further complicate the enforcement of FVIOs when both parties attend the same place of worship. Colonial legal structures designed to protect individuals from family violence do not account for these social and cultural dynamics. As a result, they often conflict with the FVIO system, exacerbating the risk of breaches and increasing the potential for further experiences of violence.

Efficacy of FVIOs in the Shadows of 'Culture'

Narratives from participants such as Mary and Akuol suggest that while FVIOs can reduce the likelihood of immediate physical violence, some victims may experience a shift in violence towards less severe, non-physical forms of harassment or abuse. These incidents often stem from within the community or extended family members, influenced by cultural norms that emphasise the privacy of family matters. This cultural disposition towards FVIOs among many South Sudanese families and individuals' conflicts with the legal framework, significantly hampering the effectiveness of FVIOs in cases of non-physical violence.

This discrepancy is particularly noticeable when compared to communities with fewer cultural pressures and less emphasis on keeping the family unit "together" and family matters away from authorities.

Participants like Mary recounted their experiences of prioritising their safety by obtaining FVIOs, yet still enduring victimisation from extended family members due to breaking cultural codes and practices. Australian law enforcement, being untrained to police such cultural dynamics, may inadvertently contribute to further victimisation. Although Australia is a multicultural country that allows individual communities to practise their culture, some cultural practices can be harmful to victims. A decolonial approach that acknowledges these practices while ensuring they are addressed within family violence cases is crucial for enhancing the effectiveness of FVIOs in Australia.

> *Mary, female participant:* We had an FVIO, but he continued to be verbally abusive afterwards. The paper did not change anything. One day, my uncle called a meeting regarding my misunderstanding with the father of my three daughters. My uncle and other family members suggested that I should go back to my husband after they had counseled him, which I did. Life continued as normal, but I still insisted that he pay my dowry because he had promised to marry me fully after I bore him children [according to tradition]. He refused to pay for my dowry and started a new relationship, so I threatened to report him to the police for violence. Since this act is against our customs and traditions, my in-laws and my husband began to disrespect my family and me.
>
> *Akuol, female participant:* The first time we had an order, he stayed away from me, but he would call and swear at me when he was drunk. I had to ask one of the elder uncles to talk to him. I reported him to my uncles instead of the police because I knew the order would not work for him.

As Mary and Akuol's accounts reveal, cultural practices that conflict with the enforcement and effectiveness of FVIOs in the South Sudanese community undermine the protection of victims and hinder the intended purpose of these orders. The fact that these women reported breaches of the order first to relatives and community elders highlights the extent to which cultural practices and internal community help-seeking intersect with legal avenues. This underscores the need to equip key community figures—such as 'uncles, aunties, and elders'—with knowledge on how to navigate the expectations of FVIOs while balancing cultural responsibilities within the community.

The majority of participants in this research reported that some breaches occurred soon after the order was granted, prior to the intervention of community elders and leaders. Morgan, Boxall, and Brown (2018) found that the risk of family violence reoffending is heightened shortly after an incident, possibly due to repeated acts of violence by controlling partners, situational factors, stressful events following the initial act of violence, or the elevated risk of violence during relationship breakdowns and experiences of shame. All these factors have the potential to undermine the deterrent effect of FVIOs.

Therefore, engaging community leaders and elders from the moment FVIOs are issued might provide wrap-around protection for victims while also offering necessary support for respondents. Understanding the circumstances in which cultural beliefs and practices intersect with protection orders is crucial to comprehending the effectiveness of FVIOs within the South Sudanese community.

Lack of Appropriate Services for Perpetrators (Respondents of FVIOs)

In many African cultures, when family violence occurs, it is traditionally the responsibility of the man's family to remove him from the family home or the wife's family to remove her, temporarily placing them with their relatives, cousins, or elders until the dispute is mediated by both families and elders within the kinship system (Juuk, 2021). This approach ensures that family issues remain within the family. However, in Australia, authorities such as law enforcement agencies intervene in cases of family violence (FV). This intervention often brings shame and stigma within the community (Juuk, 2021).

Men who are removed due to family violence face limited, if any, appropriate and available services or accommodation after being removed from their family home. This new approach to family violence intervention, coupled with a lack of proper accommodation, affects men's lives in several ways. It can potentially fuel violent behaviour towards the victim, affected family members, or even the Australian legal system, rather than rehabilitating them. Many participants spoke of losing employment due to homelessness and engaging in self-destructive activities such as substance abuse, leading to poor health outcomes, as Mabior explains:

> *Mabior, male participant:* The police arrested me, and after that, I was given a paper [referring to an FVIO] saying I was not allowed to go back home – a home that I paid for. [Deep breath…… long pause] That paper said I couldn't go home, couldn't contact her, couldn't contact the kids, or even send someone to check on them for me. Can you imagine the humiliation? I left it at that. I lost my job while moving from one place to another. I also started drinking heavily – I never drank before, only when things started to go bad. [Long pause] It's been three and a half years now, and I haven't seen the kids – they are being 'protected' from me, they said.

Experiences such as Mabior's highlight the social stigma against those removed by law, coupled with economic challenges such as job loss. These are among the many issues identified with the use of Family Violence Intervention Orders (FVIOs) as a solution to family violence perpetration. Such challenges make FVIOs a temporary solution to family violence within many African communities.

However, I acknowledge that having an order might create a much-needed gap between the respondent and the applicant. Yet, without additional support that is culturally sensitive and caters to specific community practices and beliefs, people may revert to traditional approaches to family violence—discussed in Chapter 4—which may resolve or conflict with the enforcement of FVIOs and risk the continuation of violence.

> *Mabior, male participant:* They cannot stand on their own. The shock can be so intense that it might disable them [male respondents] mentally – rendering them unable to work, and you find them just wandering aimlessly. So, yes, there are issues with intervention orders for men.

Mabior's account reveals that, while it is crucial to ensure the correct process is followed when obtaining an FVIO to prevent violence and protect victims (applicants), it is also essential to consider what happens during and after the FVIO period for perpetrators (respondents). Specifically, it is important to examine the availability and effectiveness of perpetrator programs during the FVIO period.

Male participants in this research who were referred to an intervention programs (men's group) described these programs as inaccessible due to language barriers and irrelevant because of a lack of awareness or openness to understanding the intersectional issues facing South Sudanese men, as explained by Atem below:

> *Atem, male participant:* I attended the groups they run for men, but I felt that the facilitator had no idea how deep my problems were. He just kept talking about how we should not choose violence. I wanted to say, 'Bro, violence is not my only issue; you don't know what I have been through before coming here and while here.'

Participants such as Atem emphasised the lack of access to holistic and appropriate services that cater to their psychological needs, family dynamics, cultural factors, and legal requirements during and after FVIOs. In the previous chapter, I identified the cultural, socioeconomic, and psychological challenges that drive family violence in the South Sudanese community, namely acculturation, gender roles, resource limitations, and trauma. However, these drivers are not adequately reflected in perpetrator (FVIO respondent) intervention programs during and after FVIOs (Lu et al., 2020).

Most perpetrators in this research reported having no appropriate support services to help them transition from violence to non-violence post-FVIO. This lack of support creates a sense of triple punishment: (1) legal intervention via FVIO as a form of punishment, (2) the loss of family, employment, and accommodation as an inadvertent consequence, and (3) ostracisation from extended family and the community, potentially leading perpetrators into a spiral of dysfunction, self-harm, and continued violence towards others. The isolation experienced while on FVIOs contributed to a downward spiral for respondents like Mabior, who explained:

> *Mabior, male participant:* I was homeless for a while, moving from one relative's house to another until I found shared accommodation. I had lost everything, and I was alone. It was a bad situation.

Similar to Mabior, Deng's account of his experience while on an FVIO reveals that South Sudanese male respondents are at risk of homelessness—or become homeless—due to being removed from the family home. This, in turn, negatively affects their mental and emotional well-being, as Deng explains:

> *Deng, male participant:* A lot of things go wrong in this process; there are mental health issues. It is stressful because, as a man, you will be compelled to live in either shared or rented accommodation after the intervention order. Maybe your finances won't be sufficient to cover that. You'll be exposed to different people. You may end up living in shared accommodation, where some residents are drug addicts or violent individuals, and you'll have no choice but to live with them because you have nowhere else to go.

The experiences of Atem, Mabior, and Deng—though different in expression—highlight a common issue: a lack of appropriate services to assist perpetrators in rebuilding their lives away from the applicants and protected persons. Without support, they struggle to develop strategies to address their triggers and violent behaviours, as well as the isolation they experience.

If not managed appropriately, these complex dynamics can lead to self-destructive behaviours, which are sometimes projected onto others, perpetuating further violence. Leaving perpetrators to deal with these overlapping forms of punishment on their own only widens the gap between them, the community, victims, and society. This approach contradicts the goals of rehabilitation and reintegration, potentially leading to a cycle of continued violence.

The narratives of isolation and lack of appropriate support services among perpetrators (respondents of FVIOs) in this research align with findings from other research on violence and discrimination in marginalised communities. For example, Gómez et al. (2021) argue that a lack of systemic support further marginalises men who are already on the fringes of society—often victims of systemic violence and abuse—leading to frustration and anger. As Gilligan (2001) also found, this anger fosters rebellion against the system and is often redirected onto society at large, perpetuating further violence and abuse.

Thus, rather than effectively punishing the perpetrator, ostracisation creates men who distrust the Western legal system as a source of support. Consequently, they do not seek help or engage with programs aimed at fostering social and behavioural change, instead becoming angrier and continuing cycles of violence—both towards others and themselves.

Support services and perpetrator programs are crucial for ensuring compliance with intervention orders, which, in turn, keeps victims safe. A small number of participants who breached an FVIO were referred to the Men's Behaviour Change Program (MBCP). However, these participants expressed dissatisfaction with MBCP, as described by Sallah and Atem:

> *Sallah, male participant:* The program they sent me to, to 'change my behaviour,' was full of stereotypes. They didn't want to listen; they just talked at you, at the group, and there was no privacy either.

Similarly, Atem also experienced judgement and stereotyping from MBCP facilitators:

> *Atem, male participant:* The guy started by telling us, 'In this country, people don't behave like this and that,' and he wasn't listening to anything I was saying. After a while, I kept quiet because I realised he was only interested in talking at us.

Negative experiences like those of Sallah and Atem stem from the fact that MBCPs and similar interventions are grounded in the concept of choice. They operate on the assumption that men choose to use family violence and can simply choose non-violent options (McPhail et al., 2007). These programs aim to help men take full responsibility for their actions rather than attributing their behaviour to external or internal factors, life histories, or other people.

While this approach is important and partly true, many perpetrators struggle to see themselves as having an agency in how they respond to situations. It takes time for them to unpack their ingrained beliefs and violence-supporting narratives (Vlias et al., 2017). Though the journey towards accountability is essential, there is a risk of decontextualising it—focusing solely on individual actions while overlooking the broader social processes, psychodynamic states, economic disparities, and cultural factors (as discussed in Chapter 5) that shape these choices.

> *Atem, male participant:* We face many challenges that require attention. We arrived with many thoughts and concerns, and we are also experiencing various issues within our community and from other Australian communities. All of these matters need to be addressed if we are to tackle what is labelled as "our so-called violent behaviour.

As noted earlier in this book, it is critical to acknowledge the impact of pre-migration experiences such as war and trauma, acculturation, shifting gender norms, and the structural institutions of patriarchy in shaping men's choices. Thus, while individual responsibility is vital, it must be considered within a broader framework that addresses the social and cultural drivers of family violence.

However, the current treatment and prevention programs are largely ineffective for many South Sudanese men due to various socio-cultural factors, including differing constructions of manhood, gender norms, socioeconomic challenges, mental health struggles influenced by war and refugee camp traumas, language barriers, and a lack of understanding of the legal and governance systems. Charl explains:

> *Charl, male participant:* I was referred to this men's group that met every week, and it was a waste of time. They really don't know our problems, not even half of them. Until I came to this office [his South Sudanese social worker's office, where we conducted the interview] for support, I felt my life was going backwards. They didn't understand me.

Developing cultural safety in intervention and prevention services is crucial for fostering a broader understanding of empowerment, identity, and cultural beliefs. However, MBCP programs must also address factors such as gender identity, power imbalances, trauma-informed practice, class, race, and other intersecting inequalities—particularly in understanding the experiences of both South Sudanese victim-survivors and perpetrators.

Charl's concerns, especially when he states, "they really don't know our problems" align with contemporary critiques of Western gender theories, which shape many interventions for gender-based violence. These theories often exclude African masculinities, which are shaped by multiple intersecting factors, including African cultural frameworks and social structures.

These findings align with international studies, such as Mfecane (2018), who argues that gender theories developed in the Global North offer inadequate accounts of African masculinities because they are embedded in Western epistemologies and fail to account for the socio-historical and cultural contexts of African societies. Western gender frameworks often conceptualise masculinity through a lens shaped by individualism, liberal feminism, and Eurocentric understandings of patriarchy, overlooking the communal and relational dimensions of African masculinities. Mfecane (2018) highlights that African masculinities are deeply intertwined with historical legacies of colonialism, economic structures, and traditional value systems that differ significantly from Western contexts. Therefore, applying Northern gender theories to African experiences without critically examining their cultural and historical underpinnings risks misrepresenting or oversimplifying the complexities of masculinity in African communities.

Problems Created by a Solution: Unintended Consequences of FVIOs

The issuance of FVIOs is intended to make perpetrators realise the harm caused by their behaviour and take responsibility for their actions. However, the findings reveal that, despite Australian family law aiming to protect victims-survivors through legal orders such as FVIOs, families experiencing family violence still face significant challenges due to these interventions. The social, community, and economic consequences of intervention orders may leave South Sudanese women and their families in a perceived 'worse-off position,' as participants explain below. This perception is further reinforced in situations where women are left to care for a large family on their own, often lacking the necessary experience, language skills, or confidence to navigate the employment market, which frequently results in low-income opportunities (InTouch, 2010).

Moreover, family violence and legal interventions may lead to the involvement of other social services, such as child protection, which can result in child removal and family breakdown, as documented in existing literature (Bagshaw & Chung, 2001; Barn, 2007; Bell, 2007; Chand & Thoburn, 2005; Korbin, 2002). Child protection intervention within the African Australian communities has been a source of concern since the community's early settlement in Australia. From the outset, debates and a small body of literature have emerged regarding violence and abuse against children, particularly concerning neglect and corporal punishment, which is illegal in Australia but regarded as a form of discipline in many African Australian communities (Hatoss, 2022). These debates and ongoing research have focused on disagreements about what is culturally and legally acceptable, what constitutes violence, and when child protection should intervene (Hatoss, 2022). While these discussions are crucial, the focus here is on child protection involvement when children witness family violence and are part of Family Violence Intervention Orders (FVIOs) within the South Sudanese community.

Due to its frequent mention by almost all participants, it is important to document the relationship between family breakdown, family violence, and FVIOs within the South Sudanese community. A key issue raised by both victims (applicants) and perpetrators (respondents) of FVIOs in this research is that children witnessing violence or being at risk of victimisation have led to child protection investigations and, in some cases, removal.

On the one hand, respondents emphasise the lack of appropriate services available to them while under an FVIO. On the other hand, applicants highlight the interventions of services, such as child protection, that negatively impact the family unit. While child protection in Australia is mandated to prioritise kinship care over out-of-home care for families with available kinship support (Australian Institute of

Health & Welfare, 2024, 2025), many families from CALD communities, such as the South Sudanese, still find themselves in out-of-home care placements. This is illustrated in the experience of Adau, an FVIO applicant.

> *Adau, female participant:* Once you've experienced family violence and gone through the court process, they bring in other services that are not very supportive. In my case, I had to talk to child protection workers. They wanted to separate my family and insisted that I attend parenting classes. Imagine being told how to be a mother after raising six children!

Similarly, Thon, an FVIO respondent, also experienced child protection intervention. In his case, child protection became involved after he and his wife were subjected to an FVIO. Due to the violence witnessed by their children, Thon's wife—who had full custody at the time—was investigated by child protection, which could have resulted in her losing custody, a matter of grave concern for both parents.

> *Thon, male participant:* When we had the order, they said she was not a fit mother to take care of our three children, so child protection got involved and tried to take the kids. I had to go to court again to get custody—I had to put our differences aside because they were going to take our children away.

Adau and Thon's experiences illustrate that the consequences of well-intended legal interventions in cases of family violence extend beyond the perpetrators (respondents of FVIOs). In both cases, women who sought to escape significant violence found themselves at risk of losing their children. A recurring sentiment in these accounts is that women survivors of violence were also treated as inadequate parents—either deemed unfit to have custody of their children or in need of parental training, despite their extensive experience, often gained under challenging circumstances, including displacement and resettlement as former refugees.

In this research, most FVIO applicants reported that they were subjected to child protection investigations, or their children were removed even after the perpetrator had left the family home and no longer had visitation rights. Achan, for example, describes her prolonged court battle with child protection as she tried to regain custody of her children after obtaining an FVIO and separating from her husband.

> *Achan, female participant:* My children were taken away because of the violence my ex-husband caused. He came and was violent four times, and the police got involved and called child protection. Now, I wonder if involving the police was the right decision because look at what happened, I never got my children back, and the court keeps delaying the case.

Achan's experience highlights how seeking protection through an FVIO can lead to unintended consequences, such as child protection involvement. This creates additional barriers and systemic victimisation for South Sudanese families navigating the Australian legal system (Juuk, 2021). These systemic structures, which can sometimes be punitive, contribute to the vulnerabilities faced by South Sudanese families. While victims of family violence are encouraged to seek legal interventions such as FVIOs, when these interventions come with the risk of losing custody of their children, women become hesitant to seek help. They are forced to choose between enduring an abusive partner or reporting the violence and risking child protection involvement, as Alek explains.

> *Alek, female participant:* After my ex-husband and I received the court order [FVIO] prohibiting contact, child protection stepped in. I had a meeting with eight of them questioning my parenting skills. It was terrible. So when my daughter later experienced family violence with the father of her two children, and they took her kids away because they said she was drinking, I told her, 'You should have come to me instead of going to those services. Now your children are gone, and I'm fighting to have them placed in my care. You went to seek help, but it only made things worse.'

According to Australian family law and policies, child protection is intended to act in the best interests of the child's safety and well-being (Hatoss, 2022). This approach is designed to remove children from unsafe environments and ensure their protection from harm. However, in practice, this approach often leads to family breakdown, particularly within communities where family unity and collective responsibility are central to social structures. For South Sudanese Australian families, the forced removal of children or state intervention in family matters can be perceived as a disruption to cultural values, which prioritise family preservation, reconciliation, and community-based conflict resolution (Hatoss, 2022). As a result, women like Achan and Alek's daughter not only endure the trauma of separation but also face significant stigma and shame within their community. They may be seen as having failed in their roles as mothers, wives, or daughters, further compounding their distress. The tension between legal interventions aimed at child protection and cultural expectations of family cohesion highlights a critical gap in mainstream family violence responses, which often overlook the cultural consequences and long-term impact of such interventions on affected families.

The experiences of FVIO applicants in this book further highlight that the systemic consequences of family violence interventions are not limited to victims (mostly women) but also significantly impact perpetrators. While FVIOs serve as crucial protective measures, they also introduce complex social, legal, and psychological consequences for those subjects to them. As discussed earlier, male respondents of FVIOs expressed concerns over the lack of appropriate post-FVIO interventions, follow-ups, and support services. Many felt that intervention orders function primarily as punitive tools (this is necessary, especially when violence is at a crisis point) but should be followed up with mechanisms that address the underlying causes of family violence, such as trauma, economic stress, or cultural pressures. Without rehabilitative or culturally responsive programs tailored to their needs, respondents often struggled to navigate the aftermath of an FVIO, leading to increased isolation, difficulty reintegrating into their families and communities, and, in some cases, a heightened risk of reoffending. The absence of adequate support services for perpetrators highlights a critical gap in the current family violence response strategies, underscoring the need for a more holistic approach that not only prioritises victim safety but also facilitates meaningful change for those subjected to intervention orders.

One of the consequences of child protection involvement is the intensified stigma placed on affected family members by the broader community. Within South Sudanese communities, applicants who seek FVIOs are often blamed for bringing shame upon the family, as legal intervention contradicts traditional dispute-resolution mechanisms. Consequently, women—the primary applicants—face further ostracisation and isolation, as described by Lisa below. Meanwhile, respondents, who are removed from the family home due to FVIOs, also experience isolation.

> *Achan, female participant:* After they [child protection] took my children, I was never the same. I felt alone. I was told by many people in the community that I should not have involved the police; see what happens now when you involve the police.

Achan's experience after child protection intervention left her struggling not only with the loss of custody but also with the emotional burden of isolation from her community. In many African Australian communities, family is deeply interconnected with cultural identity, social belonging, and support networks. The removal of her child not only disrupted her role as a mother but also subjected her to significant stigma, as family separation is often seen as a failure to uphold communal and familial responsibilities. This further compounded her distress, leaving her without the emotional and practical support she once relied on. Additionally, Achan faced challenges navigating the Australian child protection system, which operates within a legal framework that may not fully recognise or accommodate cultural understandings of parenting, discipline, and family unity. The experience deepened her sense of alienation as she struggled to reconcile her cultural values with the legal realities imposed on her by state intervention. Her story highlights the broader systemic issue of how child protection measures, while intended to act in the best interests of the child, can unintentionally create long-lasting emotional and social consequences for parents, particularly those from migrant and refugee backgrounds.

Intervention Order System Response Exacerbates Experiences of Racism

As discussed above, South Sudanese men lack appropriate services before, during, and even after FVIOs are in place. This section of the thesis examines findings that build on these negative experiences and the lack of services, highlighting the profoundly shared experiences among male participants regarding racism and stereotypes during their limited interactions with service providers.

In addition to reporting a lack of adequate legal, informational, and social support throughout the FVIO process, participants expressed feeling stereotyped and treated as dangerous. They observed that existing family law should not be altered to accommodate the specific needs of South Sudanese men and their families, as these laws had existed long before their migration to Australia. This sentiment is exemplified in the words of Sallah, a participant:

> *Sallah, male participant:* There is always a lot of language I hear: 'Don't complain; these laws were set before you existed.' Even one of the individuals I spoke to during my process said, 'Sallah, this law was established before you moved in. This law is to punish you violent men.' I replied, 'Do you realise the kind of racism you are introducing into our discussion? You mean I moved in from where? And what do you mean by "you violent men"?' From there, the conversation shifted slightly. I had to control myself because I was so upset. She was speaking as if all African men are violent and should not receive support simply because the law dictates that they should be punished.

Sallah's interaction with the service provider illustrates the prevalent stereotype of South Sudanese men in Australia. As he pointed out, the provider spoke as though all South Sudanese men were inherently violent. This perspective suggests that Australian family law should remain unchanged, regardless of the unique challenges faced by South Sudanese men. The perception that South Sudanese men are dangerous, inferior, and should not voice their concerns or challenge biases—whether in practitioners' attitudes or the legal system—resonates with Mayen's experiences. Despite using different words, participants reported similar encounters with racist remarks and judgement from both service providers and legal practitioners.

> *Mayen, male participant:* The law in this country is quite biased against Black people. Many of us—men—have migrated back home because they lost everything. And then they are seen as bad people, so they just leave.

Although Mayen highlights biases within the legal system, he also notes that the lack of fair treatment discourages full compliance with Australian laws. Mainstream legal and social services often fail to meet the needs of African men. The justice system is "white male-oriented" (Nancarrow, 2019, p. 4), which does not adequately serve marginalised men such as African men. The legal interventions and preventative measures frequently overlook their cultural backgrounds, lived experiences, and structural disadvantages. Consequently, South Sudanese Australian men are denied access to justice and support services that are culturally appropriate for them.

> *Garang, male participant:* It has been very challenging to live here and to call Australia home. The problem is not just family violence, it's the daily encounters with discrimination. Whether at work, school, university, or anywhere else, the feeling of being unwanted is a constant presence. You feel like you can't do anything because they say, 'This is our country.'
>
> *John-S, male participant:* Some of us who have been here long enough are given citizenship, yet we continue to be treated as unequal and not from here.

Both accounts highlight the experience of being judged and 'othered' by the system and its enforcers. Such experiences can hinder effective intervention strategies when working with perpetrators within African communities, such as the South Sudanese. The lack of culturally appropriate services can lead to systemic victimisation and the implementation of ineffective, stereotypical prevention programs. This further exacerbates structural discrimination, deepening the marginalisation of South Sudanese men and ultimately hindering efforts to address violent behaviour.

Legal representatives who hold negative stereotypical perceptions further contribute to these men's struggles by alienating them and reinforcing their diminished status (Australian Human Rights Commission, 2010; Fraser, 2009). While some practitioners view offences committed by South Sudanese men against women as a manifestation of hegemonic masculinity, it is also essential to consider their actions in the context of the marginalisation of lower-class, refugee Black men. Marx's analysis in *The Eighteenth Brumaire of Louis Bonaparte* (1852)—that men make their own history, but not under circumstances of their own choosing—applies to this situation, as South Sudanese men are forced to make choices within constrained circumstances.

The experiences of South Sudanese men align with those of other Black and Indigenous men in Australia. The concept of structural violence, as coined by Galtung (1969), provides a framework for understanding the social, political, cultural, economic, and historical factors that perpetuate inequality and suffering among Black men and other marginalised groups. Structural violence, which partially shapes gendered forms of violence, places vulnerable groups like South Sudanese men and women in precarious positions.

Black men are disproportionately represented in the criminal justice system, further reinforcing stereotypes that associate African Australian men with criminal activity, both within and outside the home (Coventry et al., 2015; Majavu, 2018; Shepherd et al., 2018). Therefore, the issue extends beyond gender inequality; it is a complex intersection of race, class, gender, trauma, and limited knowledge of Australian norms and family law.

Despite the gravity of these issues within the South Sudanese community—including family violence and its intersection with the legal system—academic attention to South Sudanese as well as other African Australian groups remains scarce. The qualitative interviews with FVIO applicants and respondents in this research aim to expand our understanding of family violence and FVIOs, shedding light on just a fraction of the challenges facing the broader African Australian community in Australia.

Conclusion

In this chapter, participants' experiences of FVIOs and their impact as a tool for family violence intervention were analysed and discussed. This section highlighted key issues facing South Sudanese people as part of the broader African Australian communities, for whom navigating FVIOs is particularly complex. While FVIOs can stop violence when police intervene, they also carry a heightened risk of exacerbating violence after police intervention.

Intervention orders can have unintended consequences that are not beneficial to either party—whether applicants or respondents. They may invite unwelcome intervention from services such as child protection, which has the potential to break down the family unit. Additionally, victims may become isolated from their communities and support services, while perpetrators, deprived of essential social, economic, and mental health support, may spiral further into violence. Furthermore, it has been found that intervention orders alone do not address the complex drivers of family violence within the South Sudanese community or the broader African Australian experience of intersecting forms of violence in Australia. Therefore, it is essential to pause and consider whether simply continuing the same approach in response to these challenges will lead to safer outcomes.

The lack of proper family and individual support during and after FVIOs, along with the absence of early engagement with crucial legal and support services, has detrimental effects on all parties involved—the AFM, the legal system, and the intervention order process itself. Additionally, underlying issues exist regarding the role of intervention orders in the context of family or relationship breakdowns. For instance, the ability of the parties involved to negotiate or develop meaningful, targeted conditions varies significantly, which can affect both compliance with and the effectiveness of the order.

Finally, this chapter highlights that, despite the use of FVIOs, they are often negotiated within the context of cultural practices that can influence their enforcement and monitoring. Applicants may also face challenges due to pressure from extended family members and community norms, which shape the types of interventions they consider acceptable. This can lead to the withdrawal of FVIOs and a reluctance to engage with services due to fears surrounding the disclosure of family violence and its legal consequences. In conclusion, the effectiveness of FVIOs as a legal intervention is often limited by operational, systemic, and cultural challenges. These orders are constrained not only by the legal system's structural limitations but also by South Sudanese cultural practices, which can influence how they are perceived and implemented. As a result, FVIOs may not always achieve their intended purpose of protection and intervention in family violence cases.

References

Australian Human Rights Commission. (2010). *In our own words—African Australians: A review of human rights and social inclusion issues.*

Australian Institute of Health and Welfare. (2024). *Child protection Australia 2021–22.* https://www.aihw.gov.au/reports/child-protection/child-protection-australia-2021-22

Australian Institute of Health and Welfare. (2025). *Child protection Australia 2022–23.* https://www.aihw.gov.au/reports/child-protection/child-protection-australia-2022-23

Bagshaw, D., & Chung, D. (2001). The needs of children who witness domestic violence: A South Australian study. *Children Australia, 26*(3), 9–17.

Baloyi, G. T. (2022). Marriage and culture within the context of African indigenous societies: A need for African cultural hermeneutics. *Studia Historiae Ecclesiasticae*, *48*(1), 12. https://doi.org/10.25159/2412-4265/10113

Barn, R. (2007). 'Race', ethnicity, and child welfare: A fine balancing act, critical commentary. *British Journal of Social Work, 37*(8), 1–10.

Bell, C. C. (2007). Evidence-based practice and cultural sensitivity. In *Presented at evidence-based practice and cultural competence in child welfare.*

Campbell, E., Bissett, T., Howard, A., Lewers, N., Polis, M., & Richter, J. (2021). *More than just a piece of paper: Getting protection orders made in a safe and supported way: Responding to Recommendation 77 of the Royal Commission into Family Violence*. Centre for Innovative Justice, RMIT University (pp. 1–130).

Chand, A., & Thoburn, J. (2005). Research review: Child and family support services with minority ethnic families—What can we learn from research? *Child Family Social Work, 10*(2), 169–178. https://doi.org/10.1111/j.1365-2206.2005.00367.x

Coventry, G., Dawes, G., Moston, S., & Palmer, D. (2015). *Sudanese refugees' experiences with the Queensland criminal justice system*. CQUniversity. Report. https://hdl.handle.net/10018/1238523

Deng, S., A. (2016). South Sudanese family dynamics and parenting practices in Australia. *Proceedings of the 38th AFSAAP Conference: 21st Century Tensions and Transformation Africa*. Deakin University: African Studies Association of Australasia and the Pacific (AFSAAP).

Deng, S., A. (2016a). *Fitting the jigsaw: South Sudanese family dynamics and parenting practices in Australia (Unpublished doctoral dissertation)*. Victoria University, Melbourne, Australia.

Deng, S., A. (2016b). *South Sudanese youth acculturation and intergenerational challenges*. Paper presented at the 39th African Studies Association of Australasia and the, Pacific (AFSAAP).

Elmusharaf, K., Byrne, E., & O'Donovan, D. (2017). Social and traditional practices and their implications for family planning: a participatory ethnographic study in Renk, South Sudan. *Reproductive health, 14*(1), 10. https://doi.org/10.1186/s12978-016-0273-2

Fraser, K. (2009). *Out of Africa and into court: The legal problems of African refugee*. Footscray Community Legal Centre.

Galtung, J. (1969). Violence, peace and peace research. *Journal of Peace Research, 6*(3), 167–191.

Gilligan, J. (2001). *Preventing violence*. Thames & Hudson.

Gómez, J. M., Gobin, R. L., & Barnes, M. L. (2021). Discrimination, violence, & healing within marginalized communities. *Journal of Trauma & Dissociation: THe Official Journal of the International Society for the Study of Dissociation (ISSD), 22*(2), 135–140. https://doi.org/10.1080/15299732.2021.1869059

Hatoss, A. (2022). That word "abuse" is a big problem for us: South Sudanese parents' positioning and agency vis-à-vis parenting conflicts in Australia. *Linguistics and Education, 67*, Article 101002. https://doi.org/10.1016/j.linged.2021.101002

InTouch, Multicultural Centre Against Family Violence. (2010). "I lived in fear because I knew nothing" barriers to the justice system faced by CALD women experiencing family violence.

Juuk, B. G. A. (2021). *Why is my family's dispute a legal problem?" The experience of South Sudanese Jieng families with family law in Australia (Unpublished doctoral dissertation).* Flinders University.

Korbin, J. E. (2002). Culture and child maltreatment: Cultural competence and beyond. *Child Abuse & Neglect, 26*(6–7), 637–644. https://doi.org/10.1016/S0145-2134(02)00338-1

Lu, M., Mangahas, X., & Nimmo, J. (2020). *Domestic and family violence in culturally and linguistically diverse (CALD) communities.* The University of Queensland.

Mafela, M. J. (2016). Marriage practices and intercultural communication: the case of African communities. *Southern African Journal for Folklore Studies, 24*(1), 1–9. https://doi.org/10.25159/1016-8427/1668

Majavu, M. (2018). The "African gangs" narrative: Associating Blackness with criminality and other anti-Black racist tropes in Australia. *African and Black Diaspora: An International Journal, 13*(1), 1–13. https://doi.org/10.1080/17528631.2018.1541958

McPhail, B. A., Busch, N. B., Kulkarni, S., & Rice, G. (2007). An integrative feminist model. *Violence against Women, 13*(8), 817–841. https://doi.org/10.1177/1077801207302039

Mfecane, S. (2018). Towards African-centred theories of masculinity. *Social Dynamics, 44*(2), 291–305. https://doi.org/10.1080/02533952.2018.1481683

Morgan, A., Boxall, H., & Brown, R. (2018). *Targeting repeat domestic violence: Assessing short term risk of reoffending* (Trends & issues in crime and criminal justice no. 552). Australian Institute of Criminology. https://www.aic.gov.au/publications/tandi/tandi552

Nancarrow, H. (2019). *Unintended consequences of domestic violence law: Gendered aspirations and racialised realities.* Palgrave Macmillan.

Ndlovu, G. E., & Naidoo, M. (2023). Changing Africa—Reflections on family involvement in African Christian marriage. *Missionalia, 51*(1), 5–20. https://doi.org/10.7832/50-0-505

O'Byrne, R. J. (2021). Marriage and belonging among South Sudanese Acholi refugees in New Zealand. *Journal of Immigrant & Refugee Studies*, https://doi.org/10.1080/15562948.2021.1933295

Shepherd, S. M., Newton, D., & Farquharson, K. (2018). Pathways to offending for young Sudanese Australians. *Australian & New Zealand Journal of Criminology, 51*(4), 481–501. https://doi.org/10.1177/0004865817749262

Vlias, R., Ridley, S., Green, D., & Ching, D. (2017). *Family and domestic violence perpetrator programs—Issues paper of current and emerging trends, developments and expectations*. Stopping Family Violence Inc.

8

"We Need More Than a Piece of Paper": Participants' Proposed Strategies for Family Violence Intervention/Prevention

Introduction

Building on the previous chapters, this book employs a decolonial approach to uncover specific experiences of family violence and highlight the limitations of existing colonial legal structures. These limitations can restrict effective responses to family violence and undermine agency for non-Western communities, such as South Sudanese Australians. Many participants, without prompting, have described these constraints and the judgement they experience within colonial systems. They have also proposed alternative strategies they believe would be more effective in addressing and preventing family violence in their communities.

The chapter explores these alternative approaches, focusing on participant-driven solutions when Family Violence Intervention Orders (FVIOs) prove inadequate. Both applicants and respondents expressed that FVIOs alone often fail to prevent violence effectively. This chapter discusses the specific strategies suggested by participants, which could be used alongside or instead of FVIOs. These approaches aim to reduce dependence on legal interventions while addressing the root causes of violence within families and intimate relationships. They stress the importance of developing culturally appropriate support systems that

A. K. Anyieth, *Decolonising Family Violence Legal Intervention Orders in African-Australian Communities*, https://doi.org/10.1007/978-3-031-95404-7_8

can operate independently or alongside formal Australian legal measures, including FVIOs. The chapter explores several key approaches to family violence intervention and prevention within the South Sudanese community: (1) a holistic approach to addressing the underlying causes of family violence, (2) enhancing practitioners' awareness of personal biases and systemic oppression, (3) community involvement and collaboration in intervention and prevention efforts, (4) the role of faith-based interventions and support systems, (5) encouraging self-reliance within the community, and (6) promoting community education and accountability. By examining these strategies, the chapter highlights the importance of culturally responsive interventions that align with the community's values and lived experiences. By integrating these insights, the chapter contributes to a broader understanding of culturally responsive family violence intervention and prevention strategies tailored to South Sudanese Australians. These strategies may also offer valuable lessons for other African communities and similarly marginalised groups in Australia.

Addressing Family Violence Drivers within the South Sudanese Community

Decolonising Australian family violence legal interventions not only involves re-examining and adapting legal frameworks that take into account the dynamics of individuals' communities, cultural contradictions, and better relationships with the community, while incorporating South Sudanese perspectives and practices, but first and foremost, re-examining the drivers and contributing factors to experiences of family violence within the South Sudanese community. A decolonial approach to family violence considers broader colonial histories of violence, systemic biases, and discrimination that contribute to family violence, including socioeconomic factors, class, race, poverty, housing insecurity, health disparities, and broader challenges specific to African Australians' experiences with the Australian legal system as discussed in Chapter 2.

Most victims (applicants) and perpetrators (respondents) of family violence within the South Sudanese community often experience some level of mistrust towards authorities, including the police, as discussed in Chapter 6, due to cultural barriers and negative experiences with Australian law enforcement. These cultural barriers include fear of authorities such as the police, child protection involvement, shame, self-blame, and a strong sense of breaching obligations to communal practices. These factors discourage the disclosure of family violence and exacerbate already difficult situations experienced by families. Additionally, clashes between the values and traditions of South Sudanese families and those of mainstream Australian society add further stress to these situations. The collective nature of many African societies, such as the South Sudanese community, presents additional challenges to the use of an individual-based approach to family violence intervention and prevention.

Many South Sudanese families, dealing with immediate settlement distress and other stressors resulting from migration, may also face discrimination and a lack of social connections, making it harder to navigate the unfamiliar. To ensure long-term, sustainable outcomes, interventions must be designed based on a holistic needs analysis of the community and individual families, with extensive community engagement and involvement. A whole-community approach nurtures relationships within the community, which are useful for both intervention and access to trusted internal support. Such an approach is particularly effective when it builds on collaboration with the community instead of a top-down approach as Sarah explains in detail below.

> *Sarah, female participant*: Since our arrival in Australia, the settlement process has been challenging for the South Sudanese community. We have faced difficulties that were not present in our previous communities, especially regarding family breakdowns. Service providers must work with us, not just for us, as many organisations operate independently from the community they serve. When organisations claim they want to serve the community, they must include us in the decision-making process and genuinely involve us in their initiatives. Additionally, we must have representatives from our community within these organisations whom we can trust. For instance, if I enter an organisation and don't see anyone who resembles me or speaks my language, it can be difficult to express myself or seek support. Moreover, some existing support services do not address

> the South Sudanese community's core issues. Many services merely sustain the problems rather than resolve them, and unfortunately, some may exploit these issues for their benefit, which fosters mistrust between the services and the community. We can all benefit if the community is involved in the services' work. Often, services design programs that cater to their needs rather than the community's, raising the question: how can you effectively help people you don't understand? Organisations need to deeply understand our experiences and be genuinely part of our community to work with us.

During discussions about alternative approaches and interventions to family violence, participants consistently emphasised the importance of incorporating cultural practices and values, discussed in Chapter 4. Their suggestions centred on decolonial interventions rooted in cultural principles of togetherness, repair, safety, and harmony. For example, participants like Achol highlighted the significance of recognising and incorporating culture into almost every aspect of their lives.

> *Achol, female participant:* For us to talk about family violence prevention, everything has to return to our culture and our collective as well as individual experiences here. It is said, 'If you don't know your culture, you don't know yourself or how to solve problems around you.' Culture is paramount, and it defines who you are and how you approach things. Our culture does not condone the use of violence. All my solutions will go back to my culture.
> *Deng, male participant:* We are always together. Our culture dictates that we stay united, so sometimes when you have a legal issue with someone you are supposed to be with, it becomes culturally difficult to just remove them or yourself from a violent situation.
> *Sarah, female participant:* People in our communities still follow their homeland's practices and traditions. Until the legal system here acknowledges and collaborates with the community, rather than working against it, they will continue to struggle with the implementation of family violence intervention orders.

Most participants in this research, like Achol, Deng, and Sarah, advocate for family violence intervention approaches that align with specific South Sudanese practices rooted in cultural traditions. Participants recognise the importance of legal interventions, including involving law enforcement and using FVIOs, to immediately address violence. However, they emphasise the need for prevention work that is proactive, community-driven, and rooted in commonly shared African cultural principles and practices, rather than being reactive and punitive. Atem's perspective echoes Achol's account:

> *Atem, male participant:* Yeah, the intervention orders are good, but clearly, they are not solving anything, so why not let us use our ways too? The work should be towards trying everything that might work, not only sticking with one thing you think would work for everybody.

Atem's account reveals a desire for a holistic approach that incorporates shared methods of intervention and prevention rather than relying on a one-size-fits-all approach. While implementing this approach may require significant resources initially, the investment can prevent victims and perpetrators from re-entering the system, ensuring long-term sustainability, as discussed in the following sections.

Redefining Intervention and Prevention: Create Culturally Appropriate Responses and Interventions

Developing culturally sensitive responses and interventions for family violence within the South Sudanese community requires a careful approach that honours and incorporates the community's unique cultural values, beliefs, and healthy practices while also acknowledging the immediate safety that FVIOs provide to victims. This necessitates a thoughtful strategy that respects and integrates these cultural elements.

The findings of this research indicate that current family violence interventions, such as the use of FVIOs in isolation, are not entirely effective. They must be complemented by South Sudanese practices, alternative intervention methods, cultural approaches to family violence, as well as resources and services that support victims (applicants of FVIOs) and facilitate positive change for perpetrators (respondents). Participants in this research propose a review and potential redesign of interventions to better address the specific needs of South Sudanese victims, perpetrators, and the wider community. This does not negate the crucial role FVIOs play in ensuring immediate safety when family violence incidents occur. However, participants suggest that legal interventions should be complemented by additional services that support individuals affected by family violence, along with their families and the broader community.

Due to the strong sense of togetherness, commonality, and the collective experience of intersecting stressors within the South Sudanese community, most participants—particularly the victims (respondents of FVIOs)—did not advocate for punitive interventions. Instead, they preferred an approach that recognises individuals (offenders) as capable of change, provided they receive appropriate intervention, prevention services, and support. As Lisa and Achol stated:

> *Lisa, female participant:* People change. We have to believe that people change for the better. I know he can change, but it is difficult given the circumstances we come from and the challenges we face in this country. Things are difficult for everybody, both men and women.
> *Achol, female participant:* After he was removed, I said, "But he is still the father of my children. He still stays in contact with them, talks to them, monitors them, and sometimes they even go to visit him." The intervention was necessary to keep us safe, and I appreciate the rules put in place by the government and the court. But I don't hate him. I just wanted him to stop being violent. And I believe that with the right support, he can actually change.
> *Tina, female participant:* I wanted law enforcement and other services to support him so that he could change. If not for me, then at least for the next woman he will be with.

Participants like Lisa, Achol, and Tina recognise that some individuals are not inherently bad but make mistakes, and with the right support, they can change. Achol appreciates legal intervention but believes that appropriate services and interventions could help her ex-husband reform. Her perspective highlights the core principle of communality and togetherness, a major component of interconnectedness in the South Sudanese community. Instead of relying solely on standalone FVIOs, professionals should engage with the fundamental goodness of both perpetrators and victims to promote healthier behaviours. This aligns with the principle of healthy communities (Bent-Goodley, 2005), which fosters healthier relationships among individuals within those communities.

Additionally, participants such as Achol, Tina, and Lisa emphasised the importance of recognising and encouraging change in perpetrators by providing appropriate support.

> *Achan, female participant:* I asked them to let me have my kids after my ex-husband was removed, as I was in a good place to care for them on my own. But the judge refused. They said I was drinking, but I had stopped drinking once the violence ended. I didn't understand why they wouldn't give me a chance to look after my children when the violent person was no longer there.

Achan's account reveals that she would have preferred the judge and child protection practitioners to acknowledge her capacity for change. Supporting such transformation requires recognising the unique needs of South Sudanese men and working with them to address those needs. Practitioners should offer non-judgemental services (perhaps with a probationary period to allow individuals to demonstrate change) and strive to reinforce positive behaviours. Promoting positive change depends on providing appropriate support and services that address both the core drivers of family violence, as discussed in Chapter 3, and individuals' personal beliefs and choices.

Systemic and Practitioner Biases

As discussed in Chapter 7, negative stereotypes and biases exacerbate participants' need for strategies and responses that are embedded within their community and culture. Participants spoke about the systemic suffering they experienced while accessing FVIOs. These legal services are designed with the best intentions—to protect victims and hold perpetrators accountable for their crimes. However, they are ultimately operated by people, and individuals may sometimes bring their personal beliefs and worldviews into their practice, which may not be beneficial for certain groups in society. Such beliefs and worldviews can create damaging biases against particular communities. For instance, Achol, Garang, and John-S reveal:

> *Achol, female participant:* The way the government [legal system] operates and treats us here has not been nice—women, men, and young people; we are all suffering. You've seen what they say about the 'African community' in the news, and that is affecting the kind of treatment we receive everywhere we go here in Australia.
> *Garang, male participant:* The Australians, the people who practice the law in Australia, say that because we are all damaged by war, we are all violent and used to being violent in our country. Yes, many of us might be carrying war-related traumas, but that doesn't mean we should be treated like damaged people or criminals.
> *John-S, male participant:* They must avoid stereotyping—which means they shouldn't assume that all African men are violent. Yes, they have to avoid stereotypes.

Garang and John-S's narratives reveal that legal practitioners often hold negative, preconceived stereotypes about South Sudanese men. These biases and stereotypes hinder fair and appropriate service delivery to members of African communities, such as the South Sudanese. Moreover, such harmful ideologies prevent collaborative and potentially effective approaches to intervening in and preventing family violence within the South Sudanese community.

Negative experiences with service providers can deter both victims and perpetrators who might otherwise be willing to seek support to address violent behaviours. Sallah's experience with a service provider highlights the negative impact of racist and preconceived notions about South Sudanese men:

> *Sallah, male participant:* She was talking as if all South Sudanese men are violent and should not get support because the law says they should just be punished.

Sallah's experience with this particular service provider reflects one of the key barriers preventing perpetrators in the South Sudanese and broader African Australian communities from seeking help. Engaging individuals who cause harm in behavioural change programs (BCP) and initiatives is already a challenge, even for those who do not experience racism and discrimination. When this existing resistance is met with racist comments and judgement, South Sudanese perpetrators become even more reluctant to seek help.

This finding supports Flood et al. (2021) report on engaging men: reducing resistance and building support. Services and practitioners who work with perpetrators sometimes label those who resist help-seeking based on assumptions about their unwillingness to change. Some of these assumptions may hold truth. However, it is necessary to first step back and examine the root causes of this resistance before addressing the behaviour being resisted. As Sallah pointed out, the treatment South Sudanese men receive from service providers contributes to their resistance to seeking help and disengagement from services—services that might have otherwise facilitated personal change.

Experiences of stereotyping and practitioner bias can lead to and exacerbate discrimination against minority groups such as the South Sudanese community. This, in turn, can further hinder help-seeking among minority and marginalised groups. Participants in this research proposed strategies that legal practitioners and the broader community could implement to overcome negative stereotypes and biases.

Community Influence

In many African Australian collectivist cultures, the definition of family extends beyond the Western notion of the nuclear family. As discussed in Chapter 1, family includes parents and siblings, grandparents, extended relatives, clans, and kinship networks. These broader family structures influence relationship dynamics, shaping expectations, responsibilities, and social obligations. Within this framework, family and community approval, whether through active support or silent complicity, can play a critical role in either preventing, perpetuating, or stopping violent behaviour (Contreras-Urbina et al., 2019).

The African Australian community holds significant power in shaping identity, reinforcing cultural values, and regulating behaviour, particularly concerning social interactions and family life (Lanham et al., 2022). While individual interventions remain vital, participants in this book emphasised the necessity of community engagement in addressing collective norms and perspectives that either condone or challenge violence. Engaging the community in open discussions about family violence allows for culturally embedded solutions that resonate with community members.

One such approach is leveraging existing cultural mechanisms, such as the involvement of elders and community leaders, in mediating family disputes and fostering non-violent conflict resolution. These respected figures often serve as moral authorities within the community, guiding individuals and families through challenges. Incorporating these cultural structures into family violence intervention strategies not only strengthens their legitimacy but also provides a crucial alternative for those who may not feel comfortable seeking help from formal institutions. For individuals disconnected from mainstream support services due to fear, stigma, or mistrust, community-based interventions offer an accessible and trusted pathway to safety and resolution, as described by Ajokdit below.

> *Ajokdit, male participant:* They don't try to give the community authority, so that when something goes wrong, the community has the authority to discuss it. If they fail, then the community will be the one to write recommendations. It will write a recommendation saying, 'You, the court, now look into it, for we are unable to resolve it.' I'm sure many things would be set right.
>
> *Alek, female participant:* The community has to be a part of the change. We came here with our ways [intervention processes], and those ways have to be recognised and supported for things to work well.

In a community rooted in communal traditions, where internal matters were traditionally handled within the community, Ajokdit's account underlines the necessity of granting the community the agency and support to address issues that risk experiences of family violence before they escalate to legal involvement. Alek and Ajokdit advocate for this approach, believing it to be effective because it empowers community members with lived experiences to lead the change process, understanding what strategies work best within their community.

While acknowledging concerns that community leaders' or elders' approaches might be rooted in patriarchal practices that pressure women to remain in violent relationships, these participants emphasise the importance of providing individuals and community members with the opportunity, alongside adequate support, to address family violence on their own terms. Rather than limiting those experiencing family violence to unfamiliar options with complex and often unsustainable processes, empowering individuals within the community to handle these issues offers a more nuanced and contextually appropriate solution.

The communal approach to addressing family violence, as advocated by Alek and Ajokdit, highlights the importance of initiating interventions at community and extended family levels. Supporting a community-level approach and integrating service delivery across areas such as Men's Behaviour Change Programs, victim and social support services, and child protection enables communities to develop interventions tailored to their specific needs. This approach reinforces the message that abuse is unacceptable while promoting both accountability and support for perpetrators seeking change.

This finding aligns with Contreras-Urbina et al. (2019), who argue that collaborating with extended families to develop innovative ways to support both victims and perpetrators of violence, while reinforcing the importance of holding perpetrators accountable, sends a strong message: family violence is unacceptable, and change is achievable with support from the family, community, professional services, and the legal system.

Collective Safety

Many participants discussed the importance of collective safety within the community, which can only be achieved when the significance of South Sudanese togetherness is recognised and family violence intervention strategies are designed to work with victims, perpetrators, families, and the community. Simply removing the violent person without providing support not only sets him up for continued violence but also affects his family and community, as their interconnected nature means they would continue to experience its consequences. As Alek explains below:

> *Alek, female participant:* We are all connected in our community and culture. So we do things together, operating as one. The law should recognise that and work with perpetrators and victims—work with us—to ensure we are all safe together, not just remove the man.
> *Ajokdit, male participant:* It is very important that they involve us, the community. They can't just help us without working with us because even that is not safe. We are all safe if we work together for the safety of all.
> *Mary, female participant:* We are all suffering in this system and culture. Even the people who are perpetrating violence are suffering too, and the children are suffering too. We are all suffering because we are one.

The views expressed by Alek, Ajokdit, and Mary highlight the deep interconnectedness of individuals within South Sudanese families and culture, which is rooted in the concept of *Ubuntu*. Although participants may not use theoretical terminology, the interconnectedness they describe is distinct from the Western psychological concept of possessiveness, which often manifests in narcissistic relationships and, in extreme cases, murder-suicides. Instead, their understanding aligns with the core principles of *Ubuntu*.

Ubuntu is deeply embedded in African culture—it encompasses shared values, attitudes, beliefs, moral codes, and practices that shape daily life (Thompson & Azibo, 2003). As a concept, Ubuntu represents a set of beliefs, values, and expectations embedded in many Indigenous African traditions and collectivist cultures, promoting dependence and humanity in meeting people's needs (Schiele, 2000). Prinsloo (2000) describes it as a philosophy concerned with the *beauty* and quality of humanity—what makes a person *ubuntu*, a desirable human being who creates harmony through love and mutual care. Thus, Ubuntu advocates for harmonious interactions that benefit both individuals and their communities, guiding human responsibilities and potential development (Schiele, 2000).

Although the full meaning of Ubuntu is difficult to capture in other languages (Letseka, 2011), scholars describe it as a process of *becoming*—one's engagement with the self, fellow human beings, the environment, and the spiritual world to be recognised as a *human being* (Manyonganise, 2015; Van Norren, 2014). Mbiti (1969, p. 106) summarises this concept in the phrase: *"I am because we are, and since we are, therefore I am"*. Chisale (2018, p. 4) further captures its essence: *"Because I am ontologically connected to other people, I am therefore obligated to care for their well-being"*.

As a result, the success or failure of individuals complying with Family Violence Intervention Orders (FVIOs), as well as the safety and justice of the applicant, their family, and the wider community, are interconnected. The fate of the man and the circumstances of the woman are not isolated from each other. If legal practitioners approached family violence cases with the understanding that the lives of those involved are linked through the principles of Ubuntu (Schiele, 1997), they could provide more informed assistance, offer more holistic follow-up support, and engage more effectively with individuals from the South Sudanese community. This would ultimately lead to better service provision.

Part of the process of decolonising thinking, systems, and structures involves recognising the importance of practitioners feeling connected to their clients' outcomes. Instead of merely assuming the role of external solution providers, practitioners should work alongside the community and extended family to support change. Achan describes her experience:

> *Achan, female participant:* Yes, the police helped remove my husband, but they didn't care about what happened to my family after that. They also involved child protection, which resulted in my children being taken away. They controlled what happened and how it happened. They watched over your neck [supervised closely] and told you, *"There was violence, so we are taking the children."*

Achan's account illustrates that while the intervention of police and other human services is crucial, it is not enough to address the challenges applicants and respondents face with FVIOs. The removal of the man alone contradicts the principles of Ubuntu—family violence does not occur in isolation, nor does it solely affect one gender, even if one gender experiences it at a higher rate. The issue is linked to the overall well-being of the family and the community.

A collective approach would encourage practitioners, families, and community members—including South Sudanese men—to stand against family violence and work towards its eradication within their communities, as Sarah explains:

> *Sarah, female participant:* The good men [non-violent men] in our community need to support women and talk to the violent men about how bad family violence is. These papers [FVIOs] alone are ruining our families and our community's social fabric. We all need to feel safe.

Sarah's statement suggests that the entire community, including men, must take a stand against family violence and promote collective safety alongside legal interventions such as FVIOs. However, to do this effectively, support must be tailored to the specific needs of the South Sudanese community. This approach would ensure that victims and other vulnerable individuals receive culturally sensitive wrap-around support.

Promoting healthy forms of intersecting equality that acknowledge the broader challenges facing African families in Australia—while also addressing gender-related issues—can help ensure interdependence. Therefore, as participants emphasised, it is essential to work with law enforcement and social service practitioners, such as police officers, lawyers, judges, and social workers, to develop a better understanding of how family violence affects South Sudanese families and their collective survival, reinforcing the importance of interdependence.

Faith-Based Support

Following the need for collective safety discussed above is the role of spirituality, beliefs, and seeking support and guidance from faith leaders as a crucial component of support. The findings suggest that for many

South Sudanese people, during times when they are "religious"—especially when faced with difficult situations—seeking protection from a higher power or from individuals perceived to be connected to the higher power, whether it be God or traditional spiritual beings, is an important practice. This belief becomes particularly evident when individuals are under strict FVIO conditions, and isolated mothers struggle to manage and make sense of their overwhelming emotions.

Spirituality during challenging times is a coping mechanism that most participants described resorting to when experiencing family violence and while subject to FVIOs. Within the context of Australia's ostensibly "secular" legal institutions and governing structures, the significance of spirituality can often be overlooked. However, recognising and incorporating spirituality into the support systems for South Sudanese people navigating FVIOs has potential benefits. For instance, having access to a trusted leader for social support, relying on a church community for guidance and counsel, and receiving referrals to services trusted by faith leaders could be invaluable to those seeking assistance.

For many participants, spirituality was a source of comfort, as exemplified in the accounts of Atem, Achol, and Charl:

> *Atem, male participant:* If I didn't pray to my God, day and night, it would've been very terrible. The most painful part is that some people, even some of my family members who did not listen to my side of the story, are still blaming me for beating my wife. Only God will change them.

Similarly, Achol also expressed the role of spirituality in her life during tough times:

> *Achol, female participant:* I had to turn to church and prayer. I pray for all of them, for all the children in the world, and even for those facing challenges—in prisons and hospitals. I pray for God's mercy on all of us.

Charl highlighted the significant role his faith in God and his church played in his life while dealing with an intervention order and homelessness:

> *Charl, male participant:* I prayed to my God every night and spoke with the pastor and the brothers at church. I forgot about my many problems when we worshipped.

As these participants explain, spirituality serves as a coping mechanism for the stresses and challenges associated with family violence and FVIOs. Atem's account reveals the importance for some FVIO respondents having a space where they do not feel judged or blamed. For Achol and Charl, prayer provided a means to express love and care for others or find peace in stressful and traumatic times.

While Achol, Atem, and Charl spoke about the importance of spirituality, John-S's account highlights the role faith leaders often play in helping families manage difficulties and navigate violence:

> *John-S, male participant:* When we got the FVIO, I said, "Pastor, we have this paper [FVIO] now, and she left the house." He was very sad for us. I stopped going to church, but my wife stayed. I didn't want the pastor to have to choose between what the Bible says about not chasing away members and what this paper [FVIO] says about us not being allowed to be in the same place, so I left the church, and I had no one else. I had to take medication for anxiety.

John-S's account demonstrates the loss of access to spirituality—he stopped attending church because of the FVIO, which he associates with his mental health decline and subsequent use of anxiety medication.

The widespread revelations of sexual abuse within the Catholic Church have significantly eroded public trust in faith-based leaders, particularly because the abuse was not only perpetrated by individuals in positions of moral and spiritual authority but also systematically concealed by the institution (Rossetti, 1995; Plante & Daniels, 2004; Dreßing et al., 2019). For many survivors and their communities, the Church's failure to protect the vulnerable and its prioritisation of institutional reputation over accountability shattered the perceived integrity and moral credibility of religious leadership. This has had far-reaching implications, especially in communities where the Church plays a central role in education, welfare, and spiritual life. The betrayal of trust has led to disillusionment, declining religious participation, and scepticism toward faith-based initiatives, even those unrelated to the abuse scandals. In this context, faith-based leaders are no longer automatically seen as safe or trustworthy, which complicates efforts to engage religious institutions in social justice or trauma-informed community work. Although religious institutions are sometimes seen as remnants of colonial systems capable of perpetuating abuse, the significance of African spirituality in addressing family violence cannot be overlooked. Engaging with faith-based communities is crucial for fostering holistic family and individual support. Since colonisation, many South Sudanese people have relied on higher powers such as God for protection, particularly during difficult times with limited support. However, faith leaders' involvement in family violence intervention and prevention in Australia is often ignored. This reluctance is largely due to a well-founded fear based on past abuse of power by church leaders.

It is important to acknowledge that the Catholic Church's history concerning family and sexual violence has caused significant harm and has rightfully influenced perspectives on faith-based interventions (Truong et al., 2022). However, while some African spiritual practices can present challenges for women, seeking help from church leaders or members of places of worship should not be discouraged. Despite negative perceptions of the Catholic Church and faith-based leaders in minority communities, people still turn to them for support. Therefore, the most effective approach is to actively collaborate with faith-based and spiritual leaders, equipping them to provide safe and informed support for their members and ensuring they know when to refer individuals to external services.

For participants in this research, the role of the church and its leaders extends far beyond religiosity—it is about having a supportive community during difficult times, serving as both a social support system and a place of worship. The negative image associated with the Catholic Church has hindered collaboration with faith-based leaders, despite the fact that victims often seek their support (Truong et al., 2022). However, participants' narratives reveal that spirituality and faith-based settings play a crucial role in shaping social networks and social norms. These environments, therefore, offer valuable opportunities to foster family violence prevention efforts.

This finding aligns with the recommendations of *The Royal Commission into Family Violence* (2016), which released its findings in 2016. The commission recommended that faith leaders and communities establish processes to assess how they currently respond to family violence, including examining whether any of their practices hinder its prevention, reporting, or recovery, or whether perpetrators exploit them to justify violent behaviour (Recommendation 165).

Like John-S, Sarah's account also demonstrates the significance of faith-based support during the time she and her husband had an FVIO:

> *Sarah, female participant:* During those times [when I was experiencing family violence], I took the kids to church on Fridays and Sundays. They could play with other kids while I worshipped with my friends. We came home a little happier after that. Our pastor was very supportive. He doesn't support abuse or polygamy. He called my husband out a few times. When we got the FVIO, he checked on me regularly in church and on the phone during the week.

Sarah's experience highlights how her pastor aligned with the FVIO system's goal of preventing violence and took action to intervene. Additionally, her account reveals an important connection between faith, community, and positive mental health—she describes feeling happier after attending church. Recognising this connection within the context of faith leaders' roles suggests that faith-based interventions can help maintain community ties and facilitate mental well-being through religious practice.

In this research, participants' beliefs in God and the role of the church community in their lives during difficult times reflect the experiences of many oppressed Black African communities worldwide. Although the role of faith leadership and places of worship—particularly churches—has been a contentious topic in recent decades, spirituality, faith leadership, and churches have long served as systems of support and comfort for Black people during adversity.

For instance, in the United States, faith leaders deeply rooted in the church, such as Martin Luther King Jr., used their platforms to educate communities, resist oppression, advocate for civil rights, and provide support, hope, and a united sense of community (Adepoju et al., 2022; Kokobili, 2019; McBride, 2003). Similarly, in South Africa during apartheid, Archbishop Desmond Tutu played a vital role in speaking out against social injustices, advocating for non-violent protest, and encouraging economic pressure on South Africa. Tutu also led the Truth and Reconciliation Commission, which aimed to heal the country by investigating human rights violations during apartheid (Crethers, 2022).

These examples demonstrate the crucial role faith leaders have played in supporting and advocating for non-violence in Black communities. Therefore, when victims and perpetrators in this research call for support from faith communities and leadership, it is essential to resist the urge to dismiss their role outright.

Encouraging Self-Reliance

While the principles of equality are vital in healthy relationships, it is crucial to redefine what constitutes a healthy relationship from a cultural perspective. This redefinition should acknowledge the impact of social and economic factors, trauma, and experiences of oppression and discrimination within the South Sudanese community, as discussed in previous chapters. Within the community lies a wealth of knowledge that can be harnessed to develop informed interventions aligned with cultural norms. Instead of relying solely on Western ideologies of family units and relationships, it is essential to assist individuals within the community in identifying healthy relationships by establishing specific criteria for acceptability within the context of one-on-one relationships (Armstrong, 2010).

Furthermore, as highlighted by many participants in this research, the establishment of structures, policies, and services from within the community is a crucial aspect of self-reliance. Many family violence services and legal institutions, including courts, are located outside the community, creating a barrier to accessing appropriate support. To address this issue, community-oriented services and group-building initiatives, such as the use of a "council of elders", are necessary to foster self-reliance and sustained efforts, as Deng and Mary explain:

Mary, female participant: Elders like my father-in-law have been through so many life experiences and know how to handle family matters according to our traditions and also according to what is right and wrong.
Deng, male participant: In African cultures, most of our societies were ruled by a council of elders, and they were successful because they saw both sides of the coin, listened to both stories, and came to a conclusion—whether lose-lose, win-win, or win-lose. That is how our people used to work, and it has helped many families.

Both Mary and Deng propose alternative approaches deeply rooted in their cultural context. Mary's mention of the "council of elders" as a community resource reflects a strategy to foster self-reliance within the community. Notably, the promotion of self-reliance was also recommended by *The Royal Commission into Family Violence* (2016). The Commission recommended that CALD communities be provided with the tools and resources to empower them to address family violence within their cultural framework while also accessing mainstream service provision.

Ensuring alignment between the Commission's recommendations and the desires expressed by the participants for their community is of paramount importance. Services that base their policies and practices on community input have the potential to provide a range of culturally sensitive family violence interventions and prevention strategies. These strategies can be tailored to address the specific needs of the community. Additionally, informal processes enable community members, through their shared values and norms, to regulate individual behaviour within the community, thereby reducing the burden on formal services.

Community Education and Accountability

Community influence and communal spirit play a significant role in bolstering community education initiatives and reinforcing accountability for violent behaviours. The importance of self-reliance, interdependence, and collective survival cannot be overstated in addressing family violence within the South Sudanese community, as participants expressed. Participants such as Achol emphasised the need to acknowledge the unique ways in which African Australian individuals are affected by family violence, stressing that inclusive responses involving their communities are imperative to effectively tackle this issue.

> *Achol, female participant:* Because of family violence, most of our children and young people have lost their way of life and culture. Family violence is breaking families, and our young people are suffering. As a mother to all South Sudanese children and young people—those dying, those alive, and even those in prison—I want us to join hands and work together to be free from violence.

Achol speaks as a concerned parent within the South Sudanese community. Although the young people affected by family violence and involved in the justice system may not be her biological children, as a member of the South Sudanese community, she understands the collective pain that South Sudanese parents and young individuals endure. Given these shared experiences and traumas, Achol advocates for a collective approach to interventions and prevention strategies to address the multifaceted injustices that the South Sudanese Australian community faces in Australia.

To instigate change and empower the community, it is imperative to establish new community-based and community-led services alongside culturally relevant interventions (Wenham et al., 2022). The South Sudanese Australian community should be encouraged to draw from lived experiences and positive cultural practices to develop services capable of delivering culturally informed interventions. These services should also foster accountability for actions and provide alternatives to legal intervention. Clear protocols should be established to determine appropriate interventions and when it is advisable to involve more formal systems. Educating families about these options—through the involvement of community leaders, faith-based figures, and elders—is essential to achieving a communal approach to countering violence within the community.

Participants in this book emphasised that the South Sudanese should actively participate in determining which services and professionals provide support within their community. This approach ensures that trusted individuals can deliver the necessary assistance, fostering structural resilience and enhancing effectiveness. It is contradictory for mainstream family violence services to express concern for women while their administrative policies fail to support the development of strong families. Similar to approaches taken by Indigenous communities (Blagg et al., 2022), the South Sudanese have embraced comparable methods to explore family dynamics and develop solutions for family violence intervention and prevention. The participants in this research recognised the need for such research and the benefits it offers in generating essential evidence that can improve both the system and the community's experiences with FVIO processes.

Conclusion

This chapter has explored alternative approaches to family violence intervention and prevention within the South Sudanese Australian community, highlighting the need for culturally rooted strategies. Participants emphasised that fostering safe and healthy families requires rethinking the philosophies and methodologies of existing family violence services to ensure they align with cultural values and lived experiences. They stressed the importance of culturally informed interventions that address the complex and interconnected challenges contributing to family violence in the South Sudanese community.

The findings reveal the necessity of a holistic approach to family violence intervention—one that integrates cultural principles and actively involves the community. Participants highlighted the importance of collaboration between service providers and the community to better support both victims (applicants) and perpetrators (respondents), ensuring that interventions address the deep-rooted issues influencing violent behaviour. They also stressed the need for practitioners to recognise their own biases, particularly those related to Black and African Australian men, such as the South Sudanese, and to provide culturally sensitive responses that move beyond stereotypes.

There was a strong consensus among participants that culturally competent, community-based interventions are fundamental to addressing family violence effectively. Developing such interventions requires thorough needs assessments, active community participation, and input from those with lived experience of family violence. Participants also highlighted the importance of addressing broader socioeconomic factors—such as employment, trauma, and education—that intersect with family violence, ultimately contributing to safer and more stable families.

Participants called for creative and culturally relevant solutions that not only protect family members from harm but also promote healing, resilience, and stronger family relationships. They proposed several key strategies, including greater community involvement in intervention and prevention efforts, faith-based initiatives, policy advocacy, and the development of culturally competent legal and support services. These recommendations reflect a broader vision for addressing family violence from within the community, fostering healthier relationships, and ultimately reducing reliance on the FVIO system.

References

Adepoju, A. V., Adepoju, O. E., & Adejumo, O. A. (2022). Remembering Archbishop Emeritus Desmond Tutu, Global health equity and human right. *The Pan African Medical Journal, 41*, 14. https://doi.org/10.11604/pamj.2022.41.14.33062

Armstrong, S. (2010). Culturally responsive family dispute resolution in family relationship centres: Access and practice. A Report for Family Relationship Centres at Bankstown managed by CatholicCare Sydney and Parramatta managed by Anglicare.

Bent-Goodley, T. B. (2005). An African-centered approach to domestic violence. *Families in Society: THe Journal of Contemporary Social Services, 86*(2), 197–206. https://doi.org/10.1606/1044-3894.2455

Blagg, H., Hovane, V., Tulich, T., Raye, D., May, S., & Worrigal, T. (2022). Law, culture and decolonisation: The perspectives of aboriginal elders on

family violence in Australia. *Social & Legal Studies, 31*(4), 535–558. https://doi.org/10.1177/09646639211046134
Contreras-Urbina, M., Blackwell, A., Murphy, M., & Ellsberg, M. (2019). Researching violence against women and girls in South Sudan: Ethical and safety considerations and strategies. *Conflict and Health, 13*(1). https://doi.org/10.1186/s13031-019-0239-4
Chisale, S.S. (2018). Disabled motherhood in an African community: Towards an African women theology of disability. *In die Skriflig / In Luce Verbi, 52*(1). https://doi.org/10.4102/ids.v52i1.2375.
Crethers, G. (2022). Desmond Tutu (1931–2021). *History in the Making, 15*, Article 13. https://scholarworks.lib.csusb.edu/history-in-the-making/vol15/iss1/13
Dreßing, H., Dölling, D., Hermann, D., Kruse, A., Schmitt, E., Bannenberg, B., Hoell, A., Voss, E., & Salize, H. J. (2019). Sexual abuse at the hands of catholic clergy. *Deutsches Arzteblatt International, 116*(22), 389–396. https://doi.org/10.3238/arztebl.2019.0389
Flood, M., O'Donnell, J., Brewin, B., & Myors, B. (2021). *Engaging men: Reducing resistance and building support*. Eastern Health, Eastern Domestic Violence Service (EDVOS), and Queensland University of Technology (QUT).
Kokobili, A. (2019). An insight on Archbishop Desmond Tutu's struggle against Apartheid in South Africa [Uvid u borbu nadbiskupa Desmonda Tutua protiv apartheida u Južnoj Africi]. *Kairos, 13*, 115–126. https://doi.org/10.32862/k.13.1.5
Lanham, A., Lubari, E., Gallegos, D., & Radcliffe, B. (2022). Health promotion in emerging collectivist communities: A study of dietary acculturation in the South Sudanese community in Logan City, Australia. *Health Promotion Journal of Australia: Official Journal of Australian Association of Health Promotion Professionals, 33*(1), 224–231. https://doi.org/10.1002/hpja.491
Letseka, M. (2011). In defence of Ubuntu. *Studies in Philosophy and Education, 31*(1), 47–60.
Manyonganise, M. (2015). Oppressive and liberative: A Zimbabwean woman's reflections on ubuntu. *Verbum et Ecclesia, 36*(2).
Mbiti, J. S. (1969). *African religions and philosophy*. E.A.E.P.
McBride, J. L. (2003). *Family behavioral issues*. American Academy of Family Physicians Home Study Self-Assessment Program (Serial No. 285).
Plante, T. G., & Daniels, C. (2004). The sexual abuse crisis in the Roman Catholic Church: What psychologists and counsellors should know. *Pastoral Psychology, 52*, 381–393.

Prinsloo, E. D. (2000). The African view of participatory business management. *Journal of Business Ethics, 25*, 275–286.

Rossetti, S. J. (1995). The impact of child sexual abuse on attitudes toward God and the Catholic Church. *Child Abuse & Neglect, 19*(12), 1469–1481. https://doi.org/10.1016/0145-2134(95)00100-1

Schiele, J. H. (1997). The contour and meaning of Afrocentric social work. *Journal of Black Psychology, 27*, 800–819.

Schiele, Jerome H. (2000). *Human Services and the Afrocentric Paradigm.* Psychology Press.

Schmidt, B. (2015). Christianity as a double-edged sword in Colonial Africa. In *Africana studies student research conference.* https://scholarworks.bgsu.edu/africana_studies_conf/2015/004/1

Thompson, S. N., & Azibo, D. (2003). *Psychosocial adjustment to chronic rheumatic conditions: The role of an Afrocultural social ethos.* Carolina Academic Press Durham.

Truong, M., Sharif, M., Olsen, A., Pasalich, D., Calabria, B. and Priest, N. (2022). Attitudes and beliefs about family and domestic violence in faith-based communities: An exploratory qualitative study. *Australian Journal of Social Issues, 57*(4). https://doi.org/10.1002/ajs4.210.

Van Norren, D. E. (2014). The nexus between Ubuntu and global public goods: Its relevance for the post-2015 development agenda. *Journal of Development Studies Research, 1*(1), 255–266.

Wenham, K., Sebar, B., Lee, P., Harris, N., & Campbell, G. (2022). Intimate partner violence in the SubSaharah African immigrant community in Chicago: A changing landscape. *Epidemiologia, 3*(3), 337–352.

9

Conclusion: A Decolonial Approach for Communities with Experiences of Colonisation and Intersections of Violence Histories

Introduction

This book addresses a relatively underexplored area in scholarly research: the intersection of African Australian experiences with the law, particularly family violence intervention orders (FVIOs) within the South Sudanese Australian community, and their interactions with African cultural practices. Given the book's broad theoretical scope, it has enriched and contributed to various fields of literature. By employing a decolonial approach and framework, it offers valuable insights into the use of legal intervention in the South Sudanese Australian community for addressing family violence and related issues. This broadens the understanding of how legal and cultural dimensions intersect in efforts to prevent family violence. The following section summarises the key discussions and findings that contribute to a deeper understanding of family violence and the significance of alternative approaches in addressing it.

A. K. Anyieth, *Decolonising Family Violence Legal Intervention Orders in African-Australian Communities*, https://doi.org/10.1007/978-3-031-95404-7_9

Chapter Summaries

This book consists of nine chapters. Chapter 1 introduces the book, while Chapter 2 further establishes its foundation by discussing the Australian migration system and the experiences of African Australians in migration and settlement. It examines how factors such as colonialism, war, and pre-migration trauma have influenced migration patterns and contributed to systemic challenges like racism, over-policing, and family violence. Additionally, the chapter highlights the intersection of patriarchal gender norms, historical violence, and the ongoing struggles faced by African Australian communities.

Chapter 3 presents empirical findings on the key drivers of family violence in the South Sudanese community. It explores how acculturation, gender roles, intergenerational trauma, displacement, and economic instability contribute to violence. The chapter also examines the impact on individuals and families, community responses, and tensions between traditional intervention methods and Australia's formal justice system. Centring the voices of South Sudanese individuals, including applicants and respondents of Family Violence Intervention Orders (FVIOs), it offers a nuanced perspective on these complex dynamics.

Chapter 4 focuses on African customary law in addressing family matters, particularly family violence. It outlines the pluralistic legal systems in Africa, where customary and statutory laws coexist, and examines how these legal traditions shape conflict resolution. The chapter discusses the role of customary law in maintaining social order and its continued relevance in post-colonial societies. It also explores the intersection of customary and statutory law, analysing the implications for individuals navigating legal challenges related to family violence.

Chapter 5 discusses the effectiveness or lack of Australian family law in addressing family violence in multicultural communities. It evaluates whether the legal system accommodates the diverse needs of African Australians and other migrant communities while engaging with formal and customary legal frameworks. Despite amendments to the Family Law Act 1975, legal pluralism remains largely unaddressed. This chapter highlights gaps in the system and advocates for better integration of culturally sensitive legal approaches to support African Australian communities.

Chapter 6 presents victims' perspectives on their interactions with law enforcement during family violence incidents. It challenges common assumptions about legal remedies and highlights systemic failures within Australian policing, particularly for marginalised communities. The chapter argues that historical and ongoing racial biases contribute to mistrust, leaving many South Sudanese victims feeling unsupported. It calls for culturally responsive and effective support mechanisms to improve engagement with state systems.

Chapter 7 examines the experiences of FVIO applicants and respondents within the South Sudanese Australian community. It details their interactions with the legal system, the enforcement of intervention orders, and their preferences for more effective interventions. The chapter evaluates the strengths and weaknesses of FVIOs from the perspectives of those directly affected by family violence. Chapter 8 extends this discussion by exploring alternative approaches proposed by the participants, addressing the limitations of FVIOs. It examines strategies that could work alongside or replace FVIOs to create more effective and sustainable solutions for preventing family violence in the South Sudanese community.

In the South Sudanese Australian community, experiences of family violence and the enforcement of family violence intervention orders often trigger pre-existing trauma linked to histories of war, displacement, and systemic marginalisation (Lucia & Cecile, 2020). Many individuals in this community have endured conflict, loss, and disrupted family structures as a result of forced migration (Lucia & Cecile, 2020). The involvement of legal authorities, particularly through intervention orders, can evoke painful memories of state violence, surveillance, and social control experienced during and after the civil war. These legal processes are often unfamiliar and may be perceived as punitive, leading to feelings of cultural alienation and emotional retraumatisation, mainly when they result in the separation from family members or the criminalisation of behaviours that may be misunderstood culturally. Without complementary support services, intervention orders may not only fail to promote healing or safety but also deepen mistrust in the legal system and further fracture families already dealing with complex post-settlement stressors. Intervention orders must be applied with cultural sensitivity, trauma-informed practices, and community-based support mechanisms to address these issues effectively. The study also highlights significant issues arising from FVIOs. In the South Sudanese Australian community, the drivers of family violence are diverse and complex. FVIOs are often negotiated within the context of cultural practices, which can impact their enforcement and monitoring. Additionally, applicants frequently face challenges due to existing negative experiences with Australian law enforcement and influence from extended families and community norms, which shape the types of interventions they consider acceptable. This often leads to fear of seeking help or engaging with services, as disclosing experiences of family violence and obtaining an FVIO may have significant social consequences. Therefore, due to numerous operational, systemic, and cultural challenges, FVIOs often function in the shadows of South Sudanese cultural practices and expectations in ways that hinder their original intent and effectiveness as a legal intervention for FV.

Moreover, intervention orders exhibit unintended negative consequences for both applicants and respondents in the South Sudanese community. They often invite unwelcome intervention from services such as child protection, which can contribute to the breakdown of the family unit. Victims experience isolation from both the community and support services. At the same time, perpetrators are left without essential support, such as social, economic, and mental health services, potentially worsening their circumstances and perpetuating cycles of violence. Participants also emphasised that intervention orders alone do not address the complex root causes of family violence in the South Sudanese community. The lack of adequate family and individual support during and after the FVIO process, as well as the absence of early engagement with crucial legal and support services, negatively impacts both parties, the affected family members, the legal system, and the intervention order process itself.

The Important of a Decolonial Approach

The decolonial approach in this book emphasises the long-lasting legacies of colonial violence, subsequent migration, escape, refugee resettlement, and settlement in a settler-colonial state shaped the South Sudanese legal consciousness and perceptions of themselves before, within, and outside the law. Understanding this historical backdrop is crucial for comprehending how these experiences have influenced the South Sudanese Australian community's encounters with violence before and after settlement in Australia.

The use of a decolonial approach in this book has facilitated a deeper awareness of the broader African Australian communities, particularly South Sudanese, experiences of violence both pre- and post-migration, as well as the resulting suffering. These hardships, stemming from colonialism, war, socioeconomic displacement, racial marginalisation, and intimate and societal violence, often manifest in destructive behaviours that exacerbate experiences of family violence. These struggles are intertwined with broader questions concerning victims' and survivors' needs, values, and ethics regarding their dignity.

Efforts to improve responses to family violence in marginalised communities such the South Sudanese community include advocating for a decolonial policing of FV, increasing community involvement in decision-making, and integrating traditional practices and healing methods. This means, it is essential to shift the narrative around intervention and prevention from one of enforcement to one of partnership and support. This change is crucial for rebuilding trust and effectively addressing family violence while respecting and upholding the rights and perspectives of South Sudanese Australians.

I argue that a decolonial approach is essential for effective legal interventions in family violence. Recognising and honouring the diverse experiences within a multicultural country like Australia (Juuk, 2023) is not only necessary but integral to preventing family violence. Marginalised communities, such as the South Sudanese Australian community, face unique realities of family violence—experiences frequently overlooked in mainstream discussions (De Haene & Rousseau, 2020; Maher &

Segrave, 2018). By valuing these differences, we can develop interventions that genuinely resonate with those affected, making them feel included and valued. This approach encourages us to understand family violence within a broader context, considering social, economic, and historical dynamics. Legal interventions must be complemented by social services that address the underlying causes and intersections of violence in African Australian communities, such as the South Sudanese community.

Additionally, a decolonial approach involves confronting the legacies of colonial violence (Atkinson, 2010). The impacts of historical injustices and systemic oppression continue to shape how family violence manifests today (Blagg et al., 2021). Therefore, addressing these legacies is imperative to ensure that legal responses do not inadvertently cause further harm. By doing so, the legal system can better acknowledge and address the needs of communities such as the South Sudanese. Community-led solutions are central to a decolonial approach, fostering trust and encouraging individuals to seek the support they need by prioritising the input and leadership of those most affected by family violence (García-Del Moral, 2018). Supporting community-based innovative solutions for family violence intervention and prevention can shift the focus from crisis management to long-term and sustainable prevention within the South Sudanese Australian community and other communities with similar backgrounds. This approach can, in addition, foster a sense of belonging and acceptance within the broader Australian society and might aid help-seeking.

Decolonisation necessitates ongoing dialogue among the community, government, police, and judicial officers about the role of traditional mechanisms as either a complementary or alternative approach to Family Violence Intervention Orders (FVIOs). This ongoing dialogue is crucial for understanding the diverse perspectives and needs. Participants consistently expressed that the community and legal practitioners should be actively involved in designing and implementing local family violence strategies. Policies should prioritise keeping families together rather than breaking them apart, which in most cases is one of the unintended outcomes of the mainstream legal approach that relies on FVIOs.

Methodological and Ethical Contributions

A decolonial methodological approach to family violence intervention, as discussed in this book, emphasises the lived experiences of participants as a primary source of knowledge (Manzo et al., 2020; Quinless, 2021; Smith, 1999). By focusing on their narratives, the nuanced understanding of family violence within the South Sudanese community is better captured and addressed. Personal stories deeply rooted in African traditions serve as a method of knowledge transmission and a means of healing, allowing survivors and community members to share their experiences in culturally meaningful ways. This methodology challenges dominant Western research paradigms, which often prioritise quantitative data over lived realities, thereby highlighting the significance of subjective experiences, cultural memory, and collective knowledge in shaping effective responses to family violence (Quinless, 2021; Smith, 1999).

The Western legal framework for addressing family violence tends to be rigid and punitive, heavily reliant on policing, court intervention, and carceral solutions (Bulbeck, 2003; Fluri & Piedalue, 2017). In contrast, traditional conflict resolution and mediation practices remain essential for managing interpersonal and family disputes within African Australian communities (Juuk, 2023). These practices prioritise reconciliation, dialogue, and collective decision-making, providing additional methods for addressing family violence that sometimes clashes with Australia's legal approaches (Juuk, 2023). A decolonial perspective critiques the assumption that legal intervention orders are the sole legitimate means of addressing family violence, advocating instead for culturally embedded, restorative approaches (Smith, 2012) that consider the social fabric of African Australian families such as the South Sudanese. Involving elders, community leaders, women groups, and faith-based mediation can promote long-term safety and reconciliation rather than exacerbating alienation and systemic harm through punitive legal measures.

Family violence within many African Australian communities cannot be understood in isolation from broader historical and structural inequalities they face in Australia. Many community members have endured war, forced displacement, systemic racism, economic exclusion, and gendered oppression (Ali et al., 2023) all of which shape their experiences of and responses to family violence. Consequently, an intersectional and trauma-informed approach can recognise these complex experiences, acknowledging that gender-based violence is intertwined with racial discrimination, migration stressors, and socioeconomic instability (Anyieth, 2024). For example, as revealed by findings discussed above, South Sudanese Australian women facing family violence may grapple with fears of unintended consequences, mistrust of law enforcement, or the stigma associated with seeking help, making it difficult to access mainstream services. A trauma-informed lens ensures that responses to family violence do not re-traumatise survivors or reinforce systemic barriers but instead provide holistic, culturally relevant support that considers the complexities of migration histories and intergenerational trauma within these communities.

This approach fosters trust, ownership, and agency, empowering communities to lead interventions that reflect their values, histories, and lived experiences. By incorporating peer-led initiatives, community dialogues, and grassroots advocacy, we can ensure that family violence interventions are co-created from within the community rather than imposed from above, leading to more effective and enduring responses to violence.

Concluding Remarks

The legal system often overlooks the unique socioeconomic challenges faced by African Australian families, including unemployment, social insecurity, and intergenerational trauma from displacement, along with various other stressors related to settlement. While legal intervention in cases of family violence can be beneficial, it fails to address the root causes of such violence, which may include economic distress, mental health issues, and cultural dislocation. Without comprehensive solutions, African families experiencing violence remain trapped in cycles of harm. If these necessary changes are not implemented, the predominantly white male-oriented criminal justice system (Nancarrow, 2019) will continue to fail the South Sudanese community and many other African communities in Australia by enforcing legal responses that do not align with their lived experiences or provide meaningful protection and justice.

Efforts to improve responses to family violence in marginalised communities include advocating for culturally competent policing, increasing community involvement in decision-making, and integrating traditional practices and healing methods. The strained relationship between Australian police and African Australian communities needs to be repaired to ensure that victims of family violence can seek help safely. Years of over-policing, racial profiling, and systemic discrimination have created deep mistrust within these communities, particularly among South Sudanese Australians, making them wary of engaging with law enforcement. For victims of family violence, this mistrust poses significant barriers to reporting abuse, obtaining protection, and achieving justice. Without trust in the police, victims may fear further victimisation, misunderstanding of their situations, or even criminalisation. To mend this relationship, it is essential to implement culturally responsive policing, engage meaningfully with the community, and acknowledge past harms. By rebuilding trust, police can become a trustworthy source of protection and support, allowing African Australian victims of family violence to feel safe and empowered to seek help when needed. Additionally, it is essential to shift the narrative around policing from one of enforcement to one of partnership and support. This change is crucial for rebuilding trust and effectively addressing family violence while respecting and upholding the rights and perspectives of South Sudanese Australians.

In conclusion, adopting a decolonial approach is essential for developing effective legal interventions to address family violence. In a multicultural society like Australia, it is crucial to recognise and respond to the unique experiences of marginalised communities, such as South Sudanese Australians. This recognition is fundamental to creating meaningful prevention efforts. Unfortunately, the realities of these communities are often overlooked in mainstream discussions, which can result in interventions that do not resonate with those most affected. A truly inclusive approach must place family violence within its broader social, economic, and historical contexts, acknowledging the systemic factors that shape these experiences. Legal responses alone are not enough; they must be complemented by comprehensive social services that address the root causes of violence and its intersections within African Australian communities.

References

Ali, M. M., Shepherd, S., & Ahmed (Shiday), B. M. (2023). Promoting trust and police legitimacy in African Australian communities: A critical reflection on community engagement strategies and practical recommendations for police. *International Journal of Police Science & Management, 25*(1), 146135572211455. https://doi.org/10.1177/14613557221145593

Anyieth, A. K. (2024). *Violence & trauma healing South Sudanese families and communities.* African World Book Inc.

Atkinson, J. (2010). *Trauma trails, recreating song lines: The transgenerational effects of trauma in Indigenous Australia.* Spinifex Press.

Blagg, H., Hovane, V., Tulich, T., Raye, D., May, S., & Worrigal, T. (2021). Law, culture and decolonisation: The perspectives of aboriginal elders on family violence in Australia. *Social & Legal Studies, 31*(4), 535–558. https://doi.org/10.1177/09646639211046134 (Original work published 2022)

Bulbeck, C. (2003). *Re-orienting western feminisms: Women's diversity in a postcolonial world.* Cambridge University Press.

De Haene, L., & Rousseau, C. (Eds.). (2020). *Working with refugee families: Trauma and exile in family relationships.* Cambridge University Press. https://doi.org/10.1017/9781108602105

Fluri, J. L., & Piedalue, A. (2017). Embodying violence: Critical geographies of gender, race, and culture. *Gender, Place & Culture, 24*(4), 534–544. https://doi.org/10.1080/0966369x.2017.1329185

García-Del Moral, P. (2018). The murders of indigenous women in Canada as feminicides: Toward a decolonial intersectional reconceptualization of femicide. *Signs: Journal of Women in Culture and Society, 43*(4), 929–954. https://doi.org/10.1086/696692

Juuk, B. G. A. (2023). *Family dispute resolution from a cultural perspective.* Cambridge Scholars Publishing.

Lucia, D., & Cécile, R. (2020). *Working with refugee families: Trauma and exile in family relationships.* Cambridge University Press.

Maher, J., & Segrave, M. (2018). Family violence risk, migration status and "vulnerability": Hearing the voices of immigrant women. *Journal of Gender-Based Violence, 2*(3), 503–518. https://doi.org/10.1332/239868018x15375304047178

Manzo, R. D., Brazil-Cruz, L., Flores, Y. G., & Rivera-Lopez, H. (2020). *Cultura y corazón: A decolonial methodology for community engaged research.* The University of Arizona Press.

Nancarrow, H. (2019). *Unintended consequences of domestic violence law: gendered aspirations and racialised realities.* Cham: Palgrave Macmillan.

Quinless, J. M. (2021). *Decolonizing data: Unsettling conversations about social research methods.* University of Toronto Press.

Smith, L. T. (2012). *Decolonizing methodologies: Research and indigenous peoples.* Zed Books.

Smith, L. T. (1999). *Decolonizing methodologies: Research and indigenous peoples.* Zed Books.

Index

A. K. Anyieth, *Decolonising Family Violence Legal Intervention Orders in African-Australian Communities*, https://doi.org/10.1007/978-3-031-95404-7

The manufacturer's authorised representative in the EU is Springer Nature Customer Service Centre GmbH, Europaplatz 3, 69115 Heidelberg, Germany. If you have any concerns regarding our products, please contact ProductSafety@springernature.com

Printed and bound by CPI Group (UK) Ltd, Croydon, CR0 4YY
30/09/2026
02225216-0001